W0036025

SAGE was founded in 1965 by Sara Miller McCune to support the dissemination of usable knowledge by publishing innovative and high-quality research and teaching content. Today, we publish over 900 journals, including those of more than 400 learned societies, more than 800 new books per year, and a growing range of library products including archives, data, case studies, reports, and video. SAGE remains majority-owned by our founder, and after Sara's lifetime will become owned by a charitable trust that secures our continued independence.

Los Angeles | London | New Delhi | Singapore | Washington DC | Melbourne

LEAN CUSTOMER ENGAGEMENT

LEAN
CUSTOMER
ENGAGEMENT

SHIL NIYOGI

Los Angeles | London | New Delhi
Singapore | Washington DC | Melbourne

First published in 2016 by

SAGE Publications India Pvt Ltd
B1/I-1 Mohan Cooperative Industrial Area
Mathura Road, New Delhi 110 044, India
www.sagepub.in

SAGE Publications Inc
2455 Teller Road
Thousand Oaks, California 91320, USA

SAGE Publications Ltd
1 Oliver's Yard, 55 City Road
London EC1Y 1SP, United Kingdom

SAGE Publications Asia-Pacific Pte Ltd
3 Church Street
#10-04 Samsung Hub
Singapore 049483

Published by Vivek Mehra for SAGE Publications India Pvt Ltd, typeset in 11.5/14.5 pt Century Std- Book by Shri Vishishta Chintamani Technologies Private Limited and printed at Saurabh Printers Pvt Ltd, Greater Noida.

Library of Congress Cataloging-in-Publication Data
Name: Niyogi, Shil, author.
Title: Lean customer engagement / by Shil Niyogi.
Description: Thousand Oaks, California : SAGE, 2016. I Includes
   bibliographical references and index.
Identifiers: LCCN 2016023053I ISBN 9789385985188 (pbk. : alk. paper) I
   ISBN 9789385985171 (epub) I ISBN 9789385985195 (ebook)
Subjects: LCSH: Customer relations. I New products. I Sales. I Marketing.
Classification: LCC HF5415.5 .N59 2016 I DDC 658.8/12—dc23 LC record
   available at https://lccn.loc.gov/2016023053

ISBN: 978-93-859-8518-8 (PB)

The SAGE Team: Sachin Sharma, Priya Arora and Mayukh Lahiri

I dedicate this book to
my father, Dr Sumanta Niyogi and my mother,
Dr Sandhya Niyogi

Thank you for choosing a SAGE product!
If you have any comment, observation or feedback,
I would like to personally hear from you.
Please write to me at **contactceo@sagepub.in**

Vivek Mehra, Managing Director and CEO, SAGE India.

Bulk Sales

SAGE India offers special discounts
for purchase of books in bulk.
We also make available special imprints
and excerpts from our books on demand.

For orders and enquiries, write to us at

Marketing Department
SAGE Publications India Pvt Ltd
B1/I-1, Mohan Cooperative Industrial Area
Mathura Road, Post Bag 7
New Delhi 110044, India

E-mail us at **marketing@sagepub.in**

Get to know more about SAGE

Be invited to SAGE events, get on our mailing list.
Write today to **marketing@sagepub.in**

This book is also available as an e-book.

TABLE OF CONTENTS

PREFACE

The idea of this book and particularly the Four E framework has its origin in multiple sources of inspiration. My initial learning in the world of sales/marketing came from the nature of my work at an entrepreneurial firm. I worked closely with customers, identified their issues, and provided remedies to those problems.

With our continued expansion we made sure that each project was conducted on a comprehensive and thoroughly individualized basis, while still using successful processes and strategies.

Effectuation comes with entrepreneurship and as we grow we make every effort to be planned. Modern-day agile product development practices have led to some norms of measurement that discourages too much work upfront without getting a customer buy-in. Many places following such agile practices, however, have wrongly interpreted this lower burden of end goal as unimportance of goals in general. And that is the reason why some firms run into unlimited sprints. Adopting effectual practices can reduce burn rates and allow the entrepreneur to better manage the evolution of the idea.

Value building calls for looking at all relevant elements and designing product parameters accordingly. How do we price the product and is there a value in pricing it low? Where do we stock products and make them available? Is there value in selling items through the big box or do we just keep it online? How do we bundle with other products? Is there a value if we bundle bread and butter together and sell? How do we deliver them? Do we use a third party for delivery?

Acknowledgments

I am thankful to the faculty at the Anderson School of Management, University of California, Los Angeles (UCLA), who taught me the importance of marketing for entrepreneurs. I am particularly thankful to the marketing and entrepreneurship professors at UCLA, who were instrumental in making us carefully look through different lenses, identifying the need of customers, and building true value for clients.

Much of what I have talked about in this book has come from employees and entrepreneurs in similar companies. I am thankful to them. I am also grateful to some of the leading business influencers and thought leaders for their work to make ideas and innovations translate into better products. I am thankful to Sachin Sharma, Subhasis Mazumdar and Premendra Sharma for their constant support and inspiration for writing the book. I also want to thank Win Kang and Jack Adler for helping me at such a short notice with illustrations and edits to keep the book interesting.

The project itself followed an iterative framework with the editors sending me valuable feedback which allowed me to greatly improve the book. Thanks are due to the creative and editorial teams.

The most significant credit goes to my family. My father, Dr Sumanta Niyogi, and my mother, Dr Sandhya Niyogi—they have been the educators in my life; they not only helped build my value system but also identified what I valued. My brother, Prasenjit Niyogi, was my enabler— he facilitated building tools and skills so that I reached heights I valued. My wife, Aindrila Gupta Niyogi, was my effecter—she helped me effect some of the most import-ant value-building decisions. My daughter, Naija Niyogi, was my engager—as she always keeps me engaged.

During my explorations, I also gathered words of wis-dom and enablement from my uncle, Harbans Nakra and my aunt, Mamata Niyogi Nakra; my parents-in-law, Lali and Pushpendu Gupta; my sisters in law, Cassidy Niyogi and Aparupa Gupta, and numerous other friends, who may not have contributed directly to the text but inspired me to embark on this project.

INTRODUCTION

As the main architect who conceived the idea and built the business from ground up, an entrepreneur often believes that he thoroughly understands the business and how to run it optimally. But if this is true why don't entrepreneurs always succeed?

The lines between the product development, marketing, and sales groups are becoming lighter, particularly with evolving minimally viable products and different pricing methodologies. When do you actually sell a product—the concept or the manufactured product—and is selling a product more important than acquiring customer attention. With fast-changing customer priorities, getting close to the customer and keeping them engaged have become the most important ingredient for success. In order to maximize interaction and prolong this relationship of the entrepreneur with his customers, a constant engagement framework works the best to maximize the value of touch points.

***

Let us run through a conventional product lifecycle, representative of how a product comes in and leaves the market. We will see how the sales and marketing teams are involved with the product. The product lifecycle has four parts: introduction, growth, maturity, and decline phases. As the product moves from one lifecycle phase to another, you will notice how the engagement with the customer goes down.

During the introduction phase of the product lifecycle, the activities are focused around raising awareness of the new product and seeking early adopters. In the growth phase, marketers' activities help expand the market in the same segment or in new segments and geographies. When a product reaches its maturity phase, the marketing activity and expenditure levels get lower than earlier on in the lifecycle as the product sells itself due to the established brand and relationships. When the product is in its decline phase, the product's existing reputation and customer loyalty produces the revenues but there is a gradual disinterest. Marketing teams often tend to put either too few or too many resources here but do not consider development of a profitable replacement product or an extension of the existing product line to cover new customer interests and changed priorities. In all this, the entrepreneur does not look at increasing the lifetime value of customers by keeping them engaged throughout this cycle.

***

This book, *Lean Customer Engagement*, is a practical guidebook to develop successful businesses through an engaged customer base. It contains a wealth of information around partnering with customers to build products or close deals in a lean and agile way without wasting effort in unnecessary sales and marketing activities. The workbook format provides meaningful support for developing evolving solutions, which can be put to immediate and prolonged use. To maximize output from every customer interaction, the book contains a Four E framework that comprehensively details four key types of engagement components or engagement interactions between the entrepreneur and the existing/prospective customer: Educate, Enable, Effect, and Engage.

Educate: This component shows entrepreneurs how to better understand customers and their unmet needs.

It also helps entrepreneurs educate patrons about new products planned by the entrepreneur and how to gather meaningful feedback from clients.

Enable: By enabling prospect customers to know more about products and their uses, the entrepreneur incrementally prepares them to make a decision. Continued enabling helps entrepreneurs get closer to the needs of the customers and to test whether their business can provide the public with what they need in a manner and price that works for both parties.

Effect: This aspect focuses on where the entrepreneur identifies whether his firm is helping the customer. Are the product functionalities or delivery standards meeting key unmet needs? Is the product bringing any value to the customer, and if not, how can he change the product?

Engage: Staying engaged with the client before the sale and beyond that are crucial elements of creating and sustaining a solid business relationship, which can lead to more sales and good word-of-mouth.

I have incorporated many outcomes and experiences from entrepreneurs and industry leaders, along with research by industry leaders on this subject. There are summaries at the end of each chapter to help the reader brainstorm possibilities of constant interaction and engagement with the customers. Overall, the use of real-life examples and case studies on entrepreneurs will help readers test hypotheses and apply the appropriate resources in the correct direction.

***

According to Bloomberg, almost 80 percent of startups fail within the first 18 months.

Figure I.1 Four E Framework

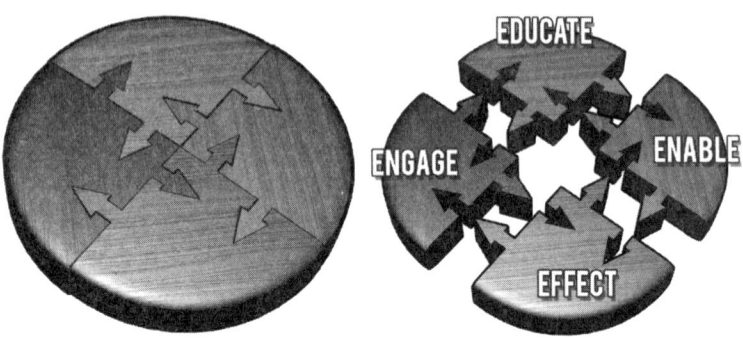

An article from Eric Wagner pointed to a study done by Bloomberg, indicating 80 percent fail within the first 18 months. According to Eric, the main reasons why businesses fail include the facts that businesses are not in touch with customers. There is no unique value in the product, there is no clear communication of the value the product brings, and there are problems with leadership and business model.

Source: http://www.forbes.com/sites#/sites/ericwagner/ 2013/09/12/five-reasons-8-out-of-10-businesses-fail/ (Accessed on November 3, 2015).

Some of the top reasons that I found include:

1. Problems with their big-picture vision
2. Issues with plans
3. Wrong or broad pain-points identified
4. Marketing to everyone rather than a specific target market
5. No financial backing

6. No plan for growth
7. No exit strategy
8. Unreliable vendors and partners
9. Lack of product diversity
10. Poor inventory management
11. Unexpected growth
12. Bad choice of "where" to do business
13. Ineffective reach
14. Bad leadership team and misaligned employees
15. Poor direction from the top
16. No idea of who the competition is nor what customers want
17. No advantage in the market
18. Lack of clarity in value propositions
19. No tried-and-tested business model
20. Low sales

You can clearly see that a vast majority of these points are related to the entrepreneur's inability to envision what brings value, and how misallocation of funds to different marketing activities can expand or sustain the business.

In this book, we will go over these areas. As we go through our Four E framework, you will see how these interactions can make your life easier.

***

John Katz was a salesman in a contingency business (e.g., if you save money for a customer, you can charge a percentage as a fee). John's forte was in understanding customers' situations by taking some samples from them and showing them how much they could save. A large part of his success was attributable to learning the ways of these customers and then educating them in different options.

As a result, John worked with customers and gave them tools and websites to enable them to change. As nobody else provided such a service in the city, he was able to effect savings for customers in a very short timeframe. This relationship, however, did not end there as John kept sending his customers more such opportunities and kept them engaged.

***

According to Forrester Research, we transitioned from the Age of Manufacturing (1900–1960, e.g., Ford) to the Age of Distribution (1960–1990, e.g., Walmart) and from there to the Age of Information (1990–2010, e.g., Google). Now we are in the Age of the Customer (2010–onwards).

We have evolved from Systems of Records to Systems of Engagement, according to Geoffrey Moore, the noted organizational theorist and author of *Crossing the Chasm*. Customers want to remain engaged in end-to-end business outcome-based solutions. The cycle times are getting shorter because companies are adapting faster, and those that take time to adapt are losing out. The companies that succeed today are those working toward customer satisfaction and focusing on educating customers, enabling them, effecting change, and engaging them.

David M. Cooperstein provided insight on how technology-fueled customer-led disruption will continue to change what businesses do as customers will want everything faster, better, and cheaper.

Source: http://solutions.forrester.com/Global/FileLib/ Reports/Competitive_Strategy_In_The_Age_Of_The_ Customer.pdf (Accessed on November 3, 2015).

Part I

Introducing the Four E Framework

Every entrepreneurial firm has three important functions. First is the generation of revenues (or sales), second is running the business and generating profits (core operations), and third is supporting these operations to sustain the business (support operations such as HR, legal, and so on). The goal of most of these firms is to keep the consumption of revenues lower than the generation—which is what makes the businesses profitable. In this book, we will talk about the first two functions—sales and core operations. The third function, though important, is increasingly being outsourced to third parties by entrepreneurial firms.

Both sales and operations depend on each other. You cannot sell a product unless it is produced by a core operations' team. Likewise, you cannot keep producing or servicing the business if you are not generating any sales. You might ask, what about doctors or engineers—are they in sales or operations? They can be a part of both. A good doctor builds a reputation (brand) and hence influences sales. At the same time, he/she performs a surgery and operates/delivers. Similarly, an engineer can both sell and deliver with his/her skill.

As we go through various professions and industries, you will see that in some cases, the operations/execution aspect is more intensive (particularly for services and complex products) while in others, sales and marketing takes the driver's seat.

***

How do sales people leverage their customer acquisition and retention skills? Does the type of product and service being sold lend itself to certain personality traits and skills? Who identifies the need, and who closes the sale? As these responsibilities differ from one entrepreneurial firm to the other, we will look into the role characteristics and where these are managed in the Four E framework.

Let us consider another example. Figaro X-ray Company markets X-ray machines (hence the name). The machines are manufactured in China and are sold in the US through sales offices in Los Angeles. Let us leave the legal and export–import aspects aside and just focus on the sales team. The sales team is headed by Hugh and the account manager is Frank. Hugh goes out and talks to clinics and hospitals and closes the sale. Once he signs the contract, he passes it on to Frank. Frank calls the customers and goes over the contract. He also checks if customers need to order anything else. Frank then assigns Carol (the installer/solution deliverer) the job. Carol also happens to have her team of project leaders and analysts.

Carol gets her work assignments on her smartphone, talks to the client, completes deployments, and comes back. She plays her guitar or watches TV, when she does not have much work. Frank, however, always remains on top of his relationship with the client and looks out for the client's needs and plans. Hugh focuses on his prospect lists and meets with Frank every week.

Another example is Kabob Times, a Middle Eastern restaurant in Chicago. The owner, Suzanne, is well known in Middle Eastern circles. She conducts belly dancing classes at the restaurant from time to time as her restaurant is also a social meeting place. The chef, Cyrus, talks to the guests, asks them about the food, takes their feedback, and incorporates those comments in his menu, thus making them contributors in the food preparation process.

In the last few months, the small restaurant space has started overflowing with customers, and hence Suzanne and Cyrus have been thinking of leasing the neighboring Chinese restaurant. They plan to open branches in New York and Boston. Cyrus has also been discussing a plan of starting a franchise and preparing a training manual for the cooks. Suzanne, impressed with Cyrus's idea, asks him to write a business plan. She also promises to give him a small equity in the business. Flash forward 10 years— Suzanne has 10 branches of her restaurant. She owns three of them and seven are franchisee owned. Cyrus has 8 percent equity in the business.

Now, let us look at the roles in the above examples. In the Figaro X-ray Company business, Frank was managing the accounts that were passed over from Hugh. Hugh was identifying the need and closing the sale and Carol was managing implementations. An account manager such as Frank is typically doing the job of an engager, while Hugh is doing the role of an effecter. Carol, who is involved in the need fulfillment with tools and products, works very closely with Frank to ensure that the client is well engaged—so she is also an engager.

In the second example, Suzanne was not necessarily closing a sale, but she was educating people about her product. She was establishing the brand of the product, and then she was connecting with customers in multiple

Figure 1.1 Kabob Times Was Started as a Small Middle-eastern Restaurant and Went on to Become a Large Organization Through Engagement

ways, thus enabling the prospects to be long-term product consumers. She was both an educator and an enabler.

Cyrus was a cook in charge of the service/product delivery. At the same time, he was keeping the customers happy and getting their feedback, thus engaging them in the process. To the franchisees, however, Cyrus was the enabler, helping them to sell and grow the account. So, you see, multiple roles can be performed by the same person for different lines. In the same vein, some roles are better defined in one industry versus another.

Further, from these examples, we see that need of marketing and sales is contingent upon the types of businesses, where and when the value gets introduced, and alignment of the organization and the customer. In other words, with changing market needs, customer priorities, business models, and responsibilities, the marketing and sales roles in entrepreneurial firms are not set roles anymore. They are not defined by personality traits and quotas. Rather, they are becoming dynamically changing, interwoven functional responsibilities within organizations, and are evolving with the engagement phase the prospective customers are in.

Let us now look at an engineering design firm, working on construction design—ABC Engineering.

At ABC Engineering, the education is conducted by the individual who identifies the pain point of the customer. The enabler works closely with the educator, builds the brand of the engineering firm, works with existing accounts, and collects success stories to influence the next prospect. The effecter here works on getting pre-sales demonstrations as well as interacting with the prospect in other ways to close the deal. And then the engager delivers the solution. So, everyone here works toward the common goal of constantly interacting with the customers and keeping the customer informed.

What we see then is a model in which the roles change as per the customer engagement needs of the industry. The calm and collected salesperson is no longer assigned to managing accounts or advancing the existing relationships. Neither do we see the aggressive salesman working individually in closing new accounts.

As we describe more about the individual components of the framework in the next chapters, we will also be taking a look at the roles that manage these interactive components at entrepreneurial firms. I have used both product development/design and product/service sales as end outcomes to describe the Four E framework because at the end of the day giving a value-bringing product design to the customer is as important as selling a product/service. These are coming even closer as customers have a greater say these days on what the product should be or look like before they buy or talk to their network about.

But before we begin, it is important to consider the different types of innovations, as well as what the entrepreneur perceives as value and brings to the customer.

1

ENGAGING INNOVATIONS BY ENTREPRENEURS

According to management expert Peter Drucker, business always boils down to two things—innovation and marketing.

An engaging entrepreneur does not necessarily need to be a great scientist or inventor, but certainly he has to have a product vision or an innovation bent, and a tendency of thinking differently from the norm. Innovations do not have to come through any groundbreaking research, but can emerge from a vision of how a better product or service might address some or all of the pain points and/or build value for the customer—thus starting to engage the customer. And some of these innovative ideas can come from the customers, who know the products/services or the need, inside out.

WHY DOES SLICED BREAD STILL REMAIN AN INNOVATION CORNERSTONE?

As sliced bread has always been used as a benchmark for innovations in our entrepreneurial folklores, I wanted to see why it was so engaging at the time it was created.

Somewhere in the late 1920s, the bread slicer was invented by Otto Rohwedder. Not a lot of bakeries wanted to buy the slicing equipment for two reasons:

1. Preslicing was considered to remove the freshness of the bread. Some bakers and customers may have experimented by slicing the bread with a knife the night before to save time in the morning rush hours (though not a lot of families experienced the rush hours in those days the way we do today). Naturally, retaining the freshness was more important than saving time.

2. There was a price to pay for the big slicer/packer machine, and a lot of bread-producing firms or bakeries did not find the investment to be worth it.

But when the slicer broke out into society, and the sliced-bread customer segment became *educated* about the fact that slicing did not affect the quality, customers found a solution to a tacit pain that they had endured for generations.

To further *enable* that innovation, other downstream industries grew (toasters, jellies, jams, butter, poultry and coffee, among others).

The ease of sliced bread *engaged* everyone in the US. It brought about a family ritual of sitting down for breakfast at the same time to enjoy family time before all embarked on their daily tasks. Again, everything did not happen because of sliced bread, as so many other factors and levers moved society to where it is now. However, the key idea causing us to refer to that as a benchmark is to show that a small tweak in an end product can quite deeply impact the way we live.

Figure 1.2 Innovation Cornerstone

The article from the Kansas City star, written by Paul Wenske, talked about the history of the bread slicer and how it changed lifestyles (or should I say loaf-styles). Like every major innovation of the day, many bakers did not like the over 10 feet long bread slicing invention. There were rumors that breads would grow stale too fast, and there was skepticism as to how much the consumers cared for sliced breads. But, as the adoption started, it became one of the cornerstones of innovations in the US.

Source: http://web.archive.org/web/20030812080649/ http://www.kansascity.com/mld/kansascitystar/6405440. htm (Accessed on November 3, 2015).

***

Since the days of sliced bread, however, many other innovations have come into being and have changed the way we think and carry out our day-to-day chores. In other words, they have been successful in not only educating and enabling us but have kept us engaged through the value they create for us.

Some of those innovations started as tweaks (new use cases and new methods) to an existing concept while some others were completely new concepts, never thought of before. The popular innovations in the recent years include:

- Big Box retailers (Home Depot/Walmart/Target)
- Big data and predictive analytics
- Bottled water
- Cirque du Soleil
- Component branding (Intel Inside)
- Curbside recycling
- Customer-centric business processes
- E-commerce
- Overnight delivery, hub/spoke model
- Financial technology (CDOs, pricing models, securitization, NPV)
- Franchising (logistics/replication)
- 'Freemium' business model
- Frequent flyer miles
- Graphical user interface and mouse
- Internet email and other Internet apps
- Local sourcing (for groceries)
- Microfinancing
- Micropayments
- Non-snack vending machines
- Office applications
- Outlet malls (logistics/replication—one-stop shop)

- Outsourcing
- Prepaid services
- Renting videos by mail
- SaaS (software as a service)
- Search engines
- Six Sigma, TQC
- Smartphones
- Solar farms
- Spinbrush
- Subscription pay model
- The electric guitar
- Video/audio streaming and packaging
- And several others I have missed

Figure 1.3 Greatest Innovations

Perhaps the Internet may have been the greatest invention in the last quarter of the 20th century. The Internet gave birth to numerous product and service innovations. It removed geographical distances and enabled e-tailing and outsourcing work to other countries. The Internet also brought people together (through dating and social media sites), helped them to connect to the world (news, watching streamed movies, and so on) and kept friends connected (through free emails and social networking sites).

But, the Internet would not have been engaging to the average consumer if he/she had not been enabled by personal computing. The foundation for the World Wide Web (or the Internet) was the PC. And the PC would not have been possible without microprocessor advancements.

A great entrepreneur develops on the basis of existing inventions in a field and innovates and improves on that. And the new business can keep upgrading and evolving until it reaches the maximum value point (MVP). MVP, according to me, as opposed to minimum viable product is about constant evolution of the minimum viable product until the product reaches a point where it delivers the most value to its customers when compared to other products in the market at that point in time.

It is not just important to build the minimum viable product but also to keep evolving until the product steers clear of any competing products in terms of new functions, delivery methods, or lower costs.

Let us take the case of Amazon.com. Amazon.com was created because of two other existing factors that laid out an environment for enabling that business: (a) the growth of the Internet and (b) the establishment of secure payment card transactions through the Internet. Add to that, the growing interest of firms in selling their own products on their websites.

Apple co-founders Steve Jobs and Steve Wozniak got some of their ideas together at the hobbyist clubs in the San Francisco Bay Area and then effectually started from a concept of a simple personal computer for consumers to developing it into what became an item that everyone wanted. The two entrepreneurs foresaw the need and the pain point of consumers. Their ideas had multiple sources: Some were their own and others came from HP, Xerox and other existing firms.

As necessity is the mother of all inventions, it was a good time for the PCs to come out on the market and that is what happened. Reportedly, Jobs' reality distortion field was legendary, and he believed that customers did not always know what they wanted. Jobs went on to create products that helped consumers in all sorts of ways. Later, consumers contributed to his ideas. What was important was to kickstart this continuous evolution of product(s), which continues to today at Apple and other computer firms.

So how does an innovation take place? Is it always an improvement on an existing product or is it a completely new concept? In the next section, we talk about some of the typical ways innovations take place. As we walk through different scenarios, we also highlight which of the Four Es are put to most use for different scenarios as marketing and sales are tied very closely to the innovations.

It is also important to mention that not all businesses focus on all Four Es equally. For instance, some products may focus all energies on educating and enabling and not look at effecting at all.

"FOR THE MASSES" PRODUCTS

New products always face an uphill task of getting known. Add to that, the permits and regulations that the product has to comply with to ultimately get into the hands of the consumers. And then, such products also need a critical mass of early adopters to help them cross the chasm. Such products, as a result, need more *education and effectuation*. In fact, a lot of consumer products fall into this category. As simplicity may be an important differentiator for many such new products, educating the prospects about these new options becomes an important marketing task.

Equally important is listening to customers and including some of their inputs into the product. With a lean process in place for this entire listening-doing-educating-listening cycle, the entrepreneur then builds the product versions incrementally.

Thomas Edison had invented several groundbreaking products; however, the product that made him famous was the phonograph. Others further improved upon Edison's design and improvised it to a product that was easier to produce, transport, sell, and most importantly be used by the customer. Innovators listen and incrementally build on top of the base product and create the maximum value point(s) of original innovation.

Let us take the case of Spinbrush. When John Osher started ideating about Spinbrush, he had other innovations in mind as well. After gauging the need from experience and knowledge of the industry, he envisioned a product that could be priced right (around five dollars) and still best serve the same purpose as the more expensive electric/power toothbrushes.

Osher had educated himself about the market and understood that the high prices of the existing products limited the electric brushes to a certain segment, and that they would not serve everyone. Osher had already brought to market a series of products. As a result, he became thoroughly educated about the mechanics of these kinds of products. He was already working with a candy twirler and so the idea of another business use case of the same mechanism occurred to him in the form of an affordable spinning brush. He let the design team know the cost he had in mind to manufacture the product. Effectually, he worked with his team to get the product down to the price he wanted it to come down to, and to also add testing features for the prospect customers to try and buy. Then he worked to further educate the community how the inexpensively priced Spinbrush functioned smoothly.

Osher educated himself about unmet needs and made things happen effectually. He had already made inroads in the toy industry with his inventions. He was working with a spinning candy twirler, when the application of the same mechanism for a toothbrush occurred to him in the form of an affordable spinning brush. He let the design team know the cost he had in mind to make an impact and make this product drive value for consumers.

Source: https://knowledge.wharton.upenn.edu/article/toys-and-spinning-brushes-how-john-osher-found-his-way-to-profits/ (Accessed on November 3, 2015).

Osher and his extensive education and effecting the development of the spinning toothbrush changed the toothbrush industry and made his toothbrush one of the greatest innovations ever. What Osher did was take a product from an upscale market as a base product, listened to consumer pains and what he/she valued, and then developed the product further to cater to these values and effectually that of the market.

Figure 1.4 For-the-masses Product

PARADIGM-TRANSFORMING PRODUCTS

Not all innovations are first-of-its-kind innovations. A large number of innovations center on transition from one interface to a completely new one. These innovations succeed with more focus on education and enabling interactions. With the advent of Internet, a lot of businesses that were transacted over newspaper or other media got a new interface.

Remember the popularity of videotape stores? Then came the widespread use of video cameras and subsequently, the idea of video files that could be shared and watched on computers.

It was the existence of those tools and ideas for file-sharing that gave birth to another popular phenomenon: YouTube. The seed of such a site was planted when the inventors of YouTube had difficulty sharing videos shot at a dinner in San Francisco. Chad Hurley, Steve Chen and Jawed Karim, all employees of PayPal, developed the idea of YouTube during the early months of 2005. Inspiration for such a site also came as video camera technology had evolved and its use had become widespread but sites hosting video clips did not exist. The pain point was obvious to these innovators.

At the dinner they attended, these innovators shot videos and took digital photos, but when they started uploading the results, they could not find a site that supported hosting of the videos for others to view. The programming expertise of Chen and Karim, and the sense of design of Hurley helped develop a convincing website.

YouTube was born when the first video was posted in April 2005. Word of mouth did the rest and users flocked to the website, making YouTube one of the fastest growing network of that time. Youtube.com had brought in a new paradigm to share both personal and public moments. Although the monetizing plan still needed some thought, the unparalleled popularity (due to the network-effect education through word of mouth) was certainly noticed by Google. Google bought YouTube in 2006 to expand their portfolio of offerings.

Back in the early 2000s, the video cameras became almost a necessity and every household had at least one. But the files were big and there were no sites, where people could share a video with others. Perhaps due to the high cost of data storage and limited number of ways to monetize (if one did not choose to run commercials), starting a company in that area did not promise perks to get entrepreneurs motivated. The YouTube founders saw the need, however, and rightly identified the gaps. New compression and photography technologies evolved and made it

(*Continued*)

(Continued)

easier for the founders. They educated the consumers and enabled them first to share their videos with friends. These customers then passed this onto their friends and became the evangelists for the product. And YouTube became one of the fastest growing networks of that time.

Source: http://www.telegraph.co.uk/news/uknews/ 2480280/YouTube-Overnight-success-has-sparked-a-backlash.html (Accessed on November 3, 2015).

Successful entrepreneurs are driven and have a clear understanding of the market dynamics, and thus they know how to change and develop their offerings so that market changes do not impact their revenues, but on the contrary, lead to the growth of the firm. Pricing new paradigms still, however, poses challenges as more and more freeloaders get addicted to a service and leave as soon as they are asked to pay up. Businesses have come up with "Freemium" concept to change this behavior of customers and monetize this addiction to their services.

When Jeff Bezos started Amazon.com, he had a vision of how the market would change, and how a new paradigm of consumers ordering online would benefit these consumers. He felt the pain point and knew that this would help consumers search an almost infinite selection, something that libraries and brick-and-mortar bookstores would not be able to offer. Perhaps quite a few of us might have been a little skeptical, as book buying has a lot to do with liking a book by looking at it or reading the first few chapters.

We tend to not always make a very informed analysis-driven decision when buying a book (I even impulsively buy books that discourage impulse buying). Borders and Barnes & Noble understood this consumer characteristic and embarked on a plan of experiential selling incrementally—real estate to read, a music-filled ambience and coffee stores—something that helped the readers to try all books they wanted to (as if they were in a library), without any pressure to buy anything. This became a great model for educating customers about a product and trial marketing to them.

Other mom-and-pop shops also offered a similar experience. They served as key socializing venues to meet with others and talk about business and life. They were also quick stops as well for those who wanted coffee, greeting cards and other items that did not require them to stay in the store for more than a couple of minutes.

However, Bezos envisioned how an online store could reverse that social behavior as consumers were becoming increasingly dependent on the Internet for their work (emails, document exchange, and so on), and by taking this education and awareness of possibilities further he enabled

Figure 1.5 Paradigm-transforming Products

the user to pick items from an infinite international selection from the comfort of one's own home via personal computer. With no expense to lease property for bookstores and limited staffing, Bezos could lower the merchandize prices, thus attracting the early adopters of this paradigm change. Effective customer service and lower price empowered the educated consumer to make an informed purchase decision. This model was dependent on the education component for his online venture to succeed. Bezos also relied heavily on improved confidence of consumers in commerce over the Internet.

Again, if you look at the history of bookstores in the US, even Barnes & Noble was responsible for a paradigm shift (or change of interface) when it started the trend of megastores, causing grief to the fragmented mom-and-pop businesses. It cut the number of smaller bookstores to almost half of what it was earlier. It also had the clout to get new books at a discount and pass some savings on to its customers.[1]

The Barnes & Noble model had a huge education component, which became an overnight success factor for the firm. Amazon.com took this spread further and became an almost any-book-you-can-order store and subsequently the anything-you-can-order store, thus initiating another wave. At first, books defined Amazon, but subsequently Amazon took on storewide products, from soup to nuts, giving Walmart, Target, and Sears a run for their money.

A successful entrepreneur for paradigm-transforming products understands the market and consumers intimately and also tests how changing one parameter in the equation affects the overall outcome.

---

[1] Jeff Wilke, SVP Operations at Amazon, had come to Anderson School of Management at a keynote speaking event in 2002, when we spoke about Amazon, the book retailer market and the supply chain operations of Amazon.

Figure 1.6 Paradigm-transforming

From these examples, you can clearly see how entrepreneurs educated themselves about the possibility of better ways of accomplishing the same outcome, and then accordingly educated and enabled prospective customers about these possibilities organically.

PRODUCTIZING SERVICES

Next, we can look at innovations in services. Every customer wants more service and for free: Lo and behold some companies provide just that. In some cases, the service itself is packaged as a product (e.g., application service providers (ASP) or SaaS type products charging subscription fees), packaged with the product (e.g., Home Depot's installation services) or packaged as a replicable set of processes along with the product (e.g., franchising services of McDonald's and others). These innovations are best marketed by enabling and engaging.

A lot of service firms started as outfits to provide peripheral and support functions to businesses that wanted to focus on core competencies. Several accounting and HR consulting firms began like that. Human resource needs and turnkey project requirements were fulfilled by these companies until a few years ago. Information technology also followed in the same footsteps, which is today the prime staple of several consulting firms. Now, even hardware and software resource needs are being fulfilled by these service businesses.

This development gave birth to the practice of ASP to manage a portfolio of applications in an effort to save on costs as well as provide expertise specific to the needs. Global consulting firms took that ASP model and made the service delivery remote/web accessible and standardized to leverage lower cost intellect overseas. SaaS vendors took this outsourcing strategy a step further by typically managing their own software and hardware while clients are subscribers of the service. Fee for using such a service is based on a number of factors, some of the most common ones being the number of users, number of hours served, number of transactions, and amount of data used.

This relatively low cost of setting up a new customer enables vendors to offer a freemium model in many cases. In this model, a free service is made available with bare bones functionality, while a fee is charged for enhanced functionality. Some other SaaS type applications are completely free to users (e.g., emails, mapping applications, crowd-sourced knowledge bases), with revenue being derived from advertising and other sources. These have been increasingly enabling their customers (think about your email—how long can we live without checking our emails?).

A key driver of SaaS's growth is the ability of the SaaS entrepreneurs to deliver a service that captures all facets

Figure 1.7 Productizing Services

of software, enable the customers with an easy way (no set up) of accessing services, and then engage them with a price that is competitive with on-site applications. As the SaaS entrepreneur operates under economies of scale, he is able to offer better service and more reliable applications to his customers at a low cost.

Let us talk about one such SaaS product, which a large majority of us may have used in the past or may still be using—Hotmail. The idea of creating a free email service hit Sabeer Bhatia when he was readying the infrastructure of a web-based database business that he was going to start. When Bhatia started Hotmail, he did that in a very agile manner. He did not have full clarity on the market size or even how soon that idea could be monetized. He knew a lot of Internet users could be enabled if they had access to free emails. What started was a series of ideation activities and tasks that incrementally led him and his associates to release a product that added value. The idea of a free email service (users felt enabled) got users engaged as thcy connected with other users and this cycle of engagement and enabling, and engagement of more users helped this idea and business to succeed.

> Sabeer Bhatia wanted to start a web-based database company and as he was putting together the plan, a firewall installation in the company (he worked at) created the need for a free email service—so that everyone could access email accounts through a browser. Hotmail started enabling and engaging users exponentially and got 5 million users in the first year of its existence.
>
> *Source:* http://www.rediff.com/business/slide-show/ slide-show-1-special-life-after-hotmail-for-sabeer-bhatia/ 20130121.htm#4 (Accessed on November 3, 2015).

Engaging customers using SaaS has not been limited to free products such as Hotmail, Yahoo, and Facebook. Amazon.com introduced Amazon Web Services to store data and perform some other services. Then it came up with Elastic Compute Cloud (EC2) to engage customers to run their applications in the cloud (the cloud is a network of remote servers hosted on the Internet to store, manage, and process data, as opposed to a personal computer or LAN).

Other ideas have gained similar traction. Salesforce.com launched force.com to let companies develop, build, store, and run apps. Google Apps engaged and enabled people to store documents in the cloud as well. All these companies worked on enabling the customers (with new ways of storage and application use) and engaging these customers (by keeping them interested) to maintain business growth.

***

Franchising is another easy way of productizing services or replicating standard procedures and processes by virtue of the brand strength, and enabling customers to buy the same service that they have experienced, read, or heard about. The franchised service/product reminds one of an old experience and shortens the customer engagement time (as they have fewer questions about the product quality).

Automobile manufacturers and gasoline companies were among the first to start franchising for easier distribution. Motels such as Howard Johnson came next. Franchising, though, did not become popular until the 1950s and the 1960s. Holiday Inns, McDonalds, Burger King, 7-Eleven, Wendy's, KFC, and several others started franchising then as a key growth strategy. Franchising for some of these companies was the only way of leveraging

Figure 1.8 Productizing Services—Cloud

the strength of the brand or effecting expansion and engaging customers with a uniform product or service.

Some of the subscription services, such as NutriSystem and Shave Club, would also fall under the productizing services' category as they also deliver a standard product as a service, and they enable (NutriSystem customers want to eat healthy and lose weight; Shave Club members value quick access to razors and shaving creams) and engage their customers.

PROCESS REFINEMENT

You may wonder how can an innovation that involves process refinement get customers to buy more? The answer may be *effectuation* of an entrepreneur's idea to get the end product to the customer faster, or *enabling* the customer to get the same value at a lower price or at a higher quality level.

Consider Google. There were other search engines in the market, so it was not the first of its kind. It redefined the process of searching. The company's BackRub search engine checked the backlinks to ascertain the importance of a site. The system looked at the relationships between websites and determined a website's relevance. The existing search engines had results ranked based on the number of occurrences of the term on the page. BackRub returned much more relevant results and became an overnight success. Google (from "googol"—the number represented by the numeral 1 followed by 100 zeros) was incorporated in September 1998 and in just over 12 years (in 2011), the monthly unique visitors to the Google website passed the one-billion mark.

Users were exponentially adopting Google as their primary search engine as Google had delivered or effected what the customers needed and enabled them to obtain more relevant results.

Google used PageRank, which determined a website's relevance by the number of pages, and the importance of those pages that were linked to the site. Page and Brin originally nicknamed their new search engine "BackRub" because the system checked backlinks to estimate the importance of a site. In May 2011, the number of monthly unique visitors to Google surpassed one billion for the first time.

Source: http://www.google.com/intl/en/about/company/history; http://infolab.stanford.edu/~backrub/google.html (Accessed on November 3, 2015).

Another example is FedEx/overnight delivery and the hub/spoke model. FedEx not only effected a more efficient service, but it also enabled far more companies/individuals by providing a trusted overnight shipping service for users to send documents/other material to a wide variety of destinations.

The package delivery market had gaps, and Fred Smith knew he had a solution for this. Smith identified the difficulty in delivering packages in one to two days. This motivated him to perform the necessary research for resolving the inefficient distribution system. In 1971, Smith used venture capital and inherited money to buy controlling interest in an Arkansas-based Aircraft Company. He started providing overnight delivery services for small packages within the US.

The operations grew from the Memphis International Airport in Tennessee. Offerings included overnight and envelope delivery services. The company chose to be headquartered in Memphis as this city was central to the target market cities, the weather was consistently great, and the airport was willing to make additional hangar space readily available. These advantages helped Smith to effect an efficient hub and spoke model for this service.

In addition, Federal Express's Smith effected the use of large aircrafts to achieve better economies of scale in his model. This factor, growing in importance, led him to lobby for air cargo deregulation, which then went a long way in spurring the company's growth with the use of larger aircraft. International acquisitions expanded the service network further, thus making it the world's largest full-service, all-cargo airline by 1989. Today, FedEx is a trusted name for guaranteed delivery and is one of the greatest examples of enabling firms

> During my MBA program at Anderson (UCLA), I came across a case study on Fedex and ever since then Fred Smith's entrepreneurship style has inspired me. Effectually, he managed the end outcome of his idea—an idea that came about from the perceived need in the market. Fedex has continued its enabling strategy and expanded its portfolio of services and its global footprint.
>
> *Source:* http://about.van.fedex.com/our-story/history-timeline/history/ (Accessed on November 3, 2015).

In 1896, Henry Ford built the Quadricycle—powered by a four-horsepower engine. The effectual leader went on to win a race against the top racecar driver in Detroit in 1901. The Ford Motor Company was incorporated in 1903 with cash from 12 investors.

Ford could produce only a few cars each day. Small teams assembled the cars from parts made by supplier

Figure 1.9 Process Refinement

companies. Only in 1913 did he begin to experiment with the assembly line concept by getting a significant portion of parts' production within the firm. He not only effected faster production of cars, but also helped consumers to get cars faster and for a lower price.

Ford revolutionized the world of mass production with his conveyor belt assembly line. In fact, conveyors are still being used and used in ways never imagined.

Ford's introduction of the moving assembly line reduced the chassis assembly from 12.5 to 1.5 hours. It was a revolution in manufacturing and the speed of production

(Continued)

(*Continued*)

> helped produce more cars as well as lowered the price of cars. Other industries followed suit and implemented conveyor belts in their plants as well.
>
> *Source:* http://corporate.ford.com/company/history.html (Accessed on November 3, 2015).

Ford did not invent the conveyor belt. It was already being used in mines and some other industries for transporting material over short distances. But he effected and evolved the process and applied it to the automobile assembly line, thus speeding up the production of cars. The assembly line enabled Ford to build cars more efficiently and at a lower cost for customers. Moreover, effectiveness increased as automobiles started getting delivered to the consumers at a faster rate.

> Even today the assembly lines have conveyors and stations for specific tasks (filling a cookie jar or fixing the steering wheel). Other machines (robotic arms, etc) work along with assembly lines to make the processes more efficient and inexpensive. The assembly line model has also been used in supply chain management and other resource and task intensive workflows.
>
> *Source:* http://www.apriso.com/blog/2013/07/100-years-after-ford-where-the-conveyor-belt-has-taken-us/ (Accessed on November 3, 2015).

Again, the effect aspect was very important here as Ford made the assembly line work and caused a significant improvement in the status quo.

EXPERIENCE IMPROVEMENT

Did you ever consider what happens if an innovation greatly increases the quality of experience of a service or a product? The entrepreneur spends a lot of resources on researching how to improve the experience and engagement, and hence the *education* component plays a major role here. Subsequently, the improved experience better *engages* the customers.

Entrepreneurial outfits such as GXXView, which builds Geographic Information Systems for utilities, leveraged the power of user interface design to make the interaction simple and intuitive for accomplishing user goals. GXXView created a system that was not only functional but also usable and adaptable. Good user interface design facilitates finishing the task at hand without drawing unnecessary attention to itself.

Designers specialize in different industries and build expertise by understanding user needs specific to that industry. For example, the application graphical user interface (GUI) designer as we saw in the case of GXXView application took into consideration the ease of retrieving engineering information remotely, while Figaro's much upgraded X-Ray machine designer was mindful of the commercial production costs and also made it platform agnostic so that the machine could use third party products. Ultimately, it comes down to clearly educating oneself as to what all functions and features helped the users. Or what did customers value?

It can start with getting educated on the functional requirements and addressing the needs of the users. This will require looking at how these users perform their tasks to see how the designed system (or end product) will fit in with the user activities. Care should be taken to make the interface appealing and keep the end product usable for all types of users working on the system. This may require bringing users in for inspecting and testing the usability of the product, so that all get served.

***

When Facebook started, membership was initially restricted to students of Harvard College; however, membership grew exponentially, and what was a college intranet became a household name.

So, what did Facebook do that was so different from the other existing sites?

It enabled a wider demographic. From teens to middle-aged moms, everyone could share his/her thoughts and events and more importantly connect with friends and family. In fact, these users were the ones who helped get the Facebook design to its present being.

Founder Mark Zuckerberg was willing to let Facebook go wherever the users wanted it to. He allowed games and other ways to connect. And that was how the user base kept expanding. The team listened but did not analyze or find fault in the user ideas. A very agile approach, changing the website to meet the incrementally evolving needs helped Facebook cause a network ripple effect (multiple network effects working together at the same time).

This experience improvement helped sustain every user's interest in the website, and the users never moved to other providers. At the same time, limited customization in the interface design helped maintain consistency for all users. Besides individuals, Facebook also targeted corporations and encouraged them to have Facebook pages very similar to how they had websites. Further, all Internet-connected devices (phones, computers, Smart TVs) enabled Facebook users to access and update from anywhere, making this ripple effect even broader.

This continuous reinvention contributed to the improvement in quality and the experience of customers. With improved experience, the customers became more engaged and subsequently got bundles of functionalities as these social systems of records and engagement interacted with each other.

Facebook was very agile and open in adopting what customers wanted—to the extent that the customers almost developed the website. That much skin in the game made them true evangelists. They took into consideration all that was said in the forums and ideated around applications without any rules or detailed plans.

Source: http://www.forbes.com/sites#/sites/adamhartung/2011/01/14/why-facebook-beat-myspace/ (Accessed on November 3, 2015).

***

Let us see another example. Before the Internet, newspapers played host to a variety of dating activities through personal advertisements. Then mail-order bride services came about which promoted the concept of searching for partners through pictures and letters. With the advent of the Internet, the concept of connecting people using pictures, text and communication remained the same, but the speed of doing that changed phenomenally.

Even before formal dating websites were set up, consumers were educated about the possibility of dating using newspapers, phone messaging, and then the web. With changing lifestyles due to the Internet (remote work, online universities and flexible schedules, among other things), social interaction at school and at work diminished enormously. Dating sites started becoming frontrunners in enabling people to build relationships through the Internet.

One of the first formal dating sites was Match.com, which emerged in the mid-1990s. A lot of advertising was conducted in the late 1990s, and even a movie *You've Got Mail* was made that got online dating into the mainstream.

Other websites not only matched profiles based on common interests, locations, and age among other preferences, but also provided chat rooms and forums for singles. Major players such as Yahoo joined the dating bandwagon. A few years later, a significant cannibalization from the social networking sites took place. With time, however, and through education and awareness, the stigma of connecting online disappeared. Match.com and other leading sites were not only responsible for the initial education of unexposed site users, but they also introduced more engagement within its user community by giving members better tools, choices, and events to interact more.

Bulletin boards and newsgroups helped the Internet-dating activities through personal ads. In addition, similar interest group meetings were taking place. Match.com was one of the first major Internet dating websites and was registered in 1995.

Source: http://brainz.org/history-online-dating/ (Accessed on November 3, 2015).

This was also true for Suzanne and GXXView. Both of them invested in changing user experience to get customers closer.

Figure 1.10 Experience Improvement

ACQUISITIONS AND GEOGRAPHIC EXPANSION

Entrepreneurs acquire other firms to provide more products for customers to choose from. Such acquisitions may also be done by vertically integrating with key suppliers, or even diversifying into a related or an unrelated market to broadly hedge the company's future. Hence, companies try to *enable* new customers by getting them tools that they did not have recourse to earlier and to *engage* existing customers by providing them with new products. This raises their cost to switch and helps to keep them loyal to the brand or product.

Microsoft's first acquisition started for the same reason of enabling and engaging. Microsoft acquired the rights to an operating system, QDOS (Quick and Dirty

Operating System), and helped IBM release it with IBM PCs in 1981. Microsoft also licensed MS-DOS to enable users on PC clones. That in turn enabled Microsoft to grow into a diverse software development firm.

Microsoft first licensed and then purchased an operating system from Seattle Computer Products. In 1981, PC DOS version 1.0 was shipped when IBM released their PC that year. Microsoft redeveloped the software to support other peripherals and subsequently the next version was released in 1983 with the IBM PC-XT's.

Source: http://www.computerhistory.org/atchm/ microsoft-ms-dos-early-source-code/ (Accessed on November 3, 2015).

Microsoft, from being a software producing and licensing company, later began making hardware with its Xbox. It then acquired Nokia's handset business. The company's acquisitions have helped it to offer not only software but a wide variety of hardware to its established customer base. These acquisitions are thus enabling new customers and engaging existing ones.

Google, similarly, engaged its existing customers with new services and enabled new customers with its acquisitions. Some of the products that we see from Google were actually those of the companies that were acquired. Google itself was an acquisition target for some of the leading Internet firms and so was Amazon. All these companies essentially went that extra mile to keep creating value and making a difference for their existing customers.

John Katz, the contingency business salesman, also became an acquisition target and eventually got bought

Figure 1.11 Acquisitions

out by a company. His business was acquired by a health insurance consulting firm that wanted to identify saving opportunities. The health insurance consulting firm had earlier done a pilot of this idea and had sub-contracted with a third party to do that. That pilot proved the enormous potential that this new line of business had and that is when they started looking for that ideal outfit that was inexpensive to buy but would be able to engage and enable customers well.

Katz's forte was in understanding customers' situations and engaging them. Katz company was nicely integrated into the company as the health insurance consulting firm dedicated more resources toward this new line of business and gained stability and growth through an engaged and enabled customer base.

***

Acquisitions though are typically not innovations, but provide new customers with a wider product base. With apt enabling and engagement, consumers can be more extensively brought into the fold of the parent company.

BASIC HOUSEKEEPING BEHIND ALL INNOVATIONS

Although we covered some innovation types, this is in no way an exhaustive list of all types of innovations. However, through all these examples, we saw that under different conditions (what the product does and who it serves) and at various points in the interaction lifecycle, the entrepreneur emphasizes one phase over the other to bring the customer into an engaging zone and keep him there. We will look at the engaging zone in the next chapters.

So, if you were the innovator/entrepreneur, what would those important tools and lenses be that you start with?

If you just started ideation, write down that idea or create a rough drawing to show how it functions and what kind of value it brings to the consumer of that product. In other words, define the utility of that product. As you go back and forth between your wireframes, it may be a good idea to do a web search for a product that resolves the same problem, how differently does it resolve the problem, and what is the price factor. Obviously, you will also look at how well the product and the company is doing.

You should also visit the patent site. See for yourself if your idea has already been patented by someone right before the idea struck you. You can get the search professionally done by third parties that specialize in IP search.

If your search shows that nobody has gotten even close to what you are thinking—Congratulations! This is the right time for asking questions to prototype experts and patent lawyers. In the US, you can get a provisional patent for a year, which can give you a year to test your idea with your family and friends (and even a pilot market) with a small investment. Once you are assured of the potential of your idea, start looking to get a non-provisional patent for your product.

You can use the phrase "Patent pending" before you are issued the patent. The patent examiner and you may have to go back and forth numerous times and it can take a few years to get your product patented. This will, however, give you some downtime for you to think about action plans for crossing the chasm—and then the most important question of all. How would you get your product out there—Licensing or manufacturing? Then carefully craft your Four E strategy that we will look into in the next chapters.

CHAPTER SUMMARY

The innovation examples and the broad categories of products helped us connect with what is valued by customers, and how innovators changed their product development and strategy and marketing focus to get the maximum bang for the buck. We also noticed that at various points in the engagement cycle, the entrepreneur can emphasize one engagement component over the other.

For example, the company that acquired John Katz's business focused most of its spend dollars on Enabling and Engaging and did not educate or effect much as his product and product users did not need much effecting and educating at that point. On the other hand, a company just starting up would have invested in education a lot more than the other three components.

When it came to the "for-the-masses" products, bidirectional education was a key component. For paradigm-transforming products, bi-directional education and enabling contributed to connecting with the customers. For productizing services, engaging and enabling of customers was the combination that helped. While process refinement was a lot about effectuating a change and subsequently ensuring that the customers were enabled; experience improvement focused on educating and engaging customers. New products in the portfolio due to acquisitions and geographic expansions engaged existing customers by getting them better or more tools that they did not have easy recourse to, and enabled new customers by providing them with the expanded portfolio of products.

Now, if you have already gone through all these steps, and somehow the customers do not get the value of your product and seem to not be engaged by it, the next chapters will help you reevaluate your product positioning. Pointers will be given on how to educate yourself about the changing needs of the customers, and to enable yourself with price points and delivery methods that will be most useful for making the customers realize the value of your product. We will also discuss engaging customers through various other methods.

Part II
The Framework and the Phases

From the earlier chapter, we saw how the need of marketing and sales is contingent upon the types of products and customers, how soon can the value be introduced to the customer in the product lifecycle, and how soon can the inputs from the customers get incorporated into the products. We also saw that with changing customer priorities and business models, the marketing and sales roles are becoming dynamically changing responsibilities within organizations, and are evolving with the engagement phase the prospective customers are part of. In other words, the assessment should be made as to whether the customers are in Educate, Enable, Effect or Engage phases of the sale or product development (or marketing) first and then accordingly decided as to how they should be interacted with.

Depending on the type of product innovation and also on the line of business, the entrepreneur emphasizes one phase over another. The same product, as it is evolved further, may have him refocus on a completely different phase. For example, when any product enters the market, a lot of time and money is spent on research—both customer understanding (market research) and R&D (identifying product viability). In other words, a lot of resources are dedicated to *Education*. However, if the product has been in the market for some time, people behind it start ideating around improving the experience of customers, refining the product quality, pricing it better, or increasing the reach. And, that becomes an *Enable* or *Engage* activity.

***

The more important point is to know when do you move from one stage to the other. Keep going back to the metrics but at the same time also consider changing the metrics as customers change and their tastes transform. In that case, the most important characteristic that an entrepreneur should have is openness to new possibilities. Such openness also builds positivity and creativity within an organization. After all, when we innovate or think outside the box, we may not really be doing something never done. We may be taking an established, successful concept and applying it to another place or walk of life. Or for that matter, we are formalizing a workaround that we have always used and establishing that workaround as a standard practice.

However, ideation and idea presentation is sometimes shot down by entrepreneurs, who are more focused on short-term profitability and who fail to realize that innovation also happens to be the path to long-term sustainability.

Failure still remains the stepping stone to success, and that is even applicable to those who avoid roadblocks by thinking outside the box and by being agile and doing the right thing incrementally/iteratively to get to the end point.

Figure 2.1 Four E Framework Unplugged

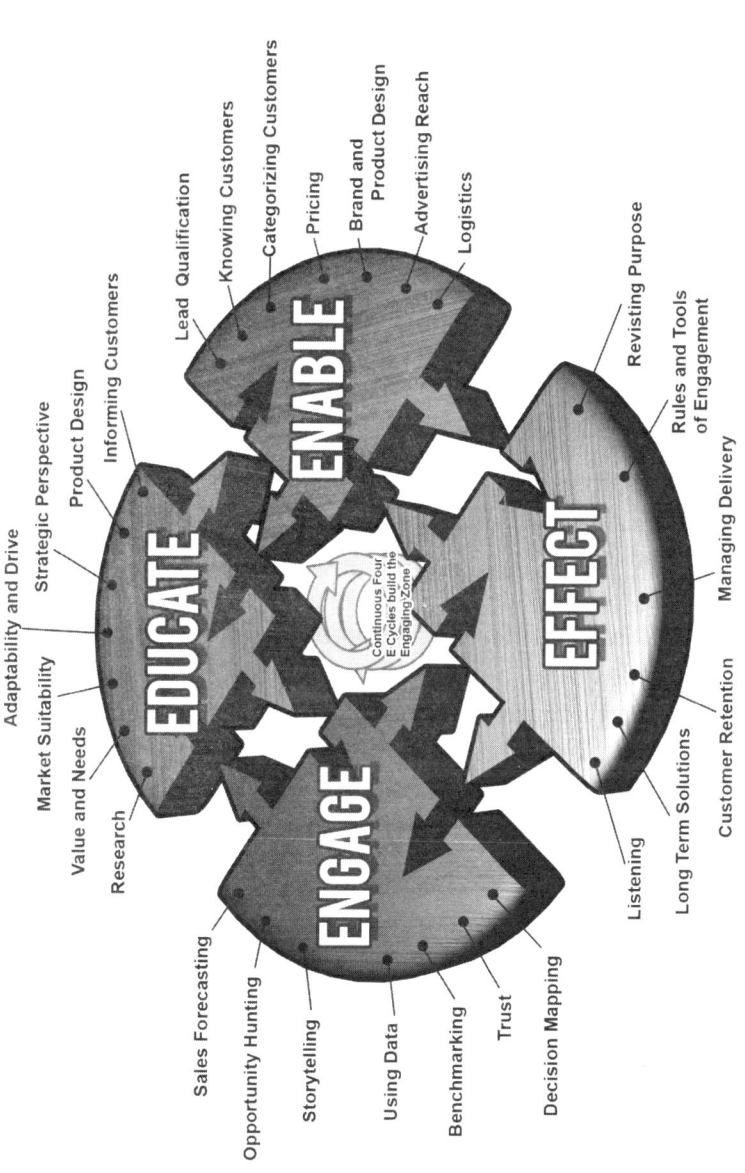

There will be failures but failing fast and learning from them is what is more important. Entrepreneurs and innovators who make it are really good at listening and interacting with other people who have knowledge and learn from their experiences. They do not believe in having to experience situations first-hand for everything, and instead keep educating themselves from all sources possible. As a result they use time and money most effectively.

Zig Ziglar, the author of several sales-related bestsellers, used to believe in changing decision patterns into habits. If you listen to a piece 16 times and you like it, then you naturally commit to it and that becomes a part of your life. This becomes even more interesting if every time you get inspired, you relate the same to a friend and he similarly likes and inspires others. This wise advice becomes his habit too. This is how easily social media can influence a product's success.

Now consider this. Einstein said that one incorrect input has to be neutralized by 11 correct inputs. So, if you receive a negative feedback about your product, you need at least 11 good reviews or inputs about your product to neutralize the impact of the negative comment. The last thing you would want is to have dissatisfied customers. If you bring these two together, you see that it takes 16 times to get someone to buy something so that it becomes a habit, whereas to neutralize a negative review it takes 11 loyalist reviews. So, we have to ensure that our customers are properly educated, enabled and engaged to see the value in our product/service, be loyal to try it at least 16 times or be super-loyal (or evangelists) to reverse a negative review from another source.

***

Mark Twain once said, "Everybody talks about the weather, but nobody does anything about it". His comment is still humorous. However, when you apply it to entrepreneurial ideas, you see a similar "nobody does anything about it" theme. Perhaps, if we hear too much talk about some of the great ideas that the entrepreneur or his employees have, then it might be important to start working on prioritizing and executing them effectually.

The Effectuate or Effect phase is about getting things done. Effect is also about being disruptive, which applies to crazy and successful entrepreneurs. In a ride filled with uncertainties, the effect component aims at prolonging the crests and reducing the occurrence and depth of troughs. Effecting is also about being a chooser and not waiting to be chosen; about being in the front seat and not being the dog in the dog-and-pony show.

The entrepreneur has tools, ideas and attitude; however, he is not sure how the customers would be best served by the product/service. Netflix started sending DVDs by mail and discovered an initial indifference of the customers in the beginning. However, as time passed, the mail option became the key differentiator from the video/DVD shops and also provided Netflix with a large advantage over them.

Think about Effect as the closing (sales) or the finalizing (product) process. In other words, folks who are deeply involved in risk taking and making it happen (e.g., Tom Brady, Steve Jobs, among others) are examples of great effecters. Effect also helps in identifying if the pursuit (sale or product development) makes any sense to be continued as it compares the actual outcome (so far) with the planned outcome.

***

A few years ago when Frank, the account manager at Figaro's, had a very bad headache while he was on the phone for a few hours with a client of Figaro's, he had asked his associate, Carol, for a headache-relieving medicine. Carol, however, asked Frank to hit the wall with a closed fist instead. On asking her how that would relieve his pain, she said that his attention would be refocused on the new pain so he would think less about his headache.

That is exactly what happens in some organizations; they keep their focus on the largest fires which decide their work prioritization. Testing disruptive ideas becomes difficult as they never provide a real list of possible products.

At agile product development shops, product ideas evolve from an idea. Once the first shipping-ready or minimum viable product is reached, the entrepreneur looks to further evolving it. The development team then prioritizes the more important product functions over the less important ones. Incrementally and effectually, the product team keeps improving the product till it gets an approval from all stakeholders and the product owner.

***

People say that they can do multiple things at the same time ("I am a multi-tasker"). However, according to psychologists, nobody can do multiple things at the same time as the brain can focus on only one thing at a time. Can you listen and speak at the same time? What you tend to do is divide the focus span into tiny time slots and alternate between the tasks (one second listening and then one second talking). But as we master this attention-balancing we feel convinced that we can multi-task.

Normally, you can still do one cerebral task and one not-so-cerebral job at the same time (e.g., talking on the phone and baking food using a timer or listening to the news while on the treadmill). Such a model requires you to trust the assurance of the not-so-cerebral job's outcome (the timer signals you to remove the food from the oven; the treadmill shows you numbers to tell you that your set is over). The cerebral job, on the other hand, is then where you put all your attention as you have to make important tactical decisions all throughout.

Now if our lives had only one cerebral job and everything else was a collection of non-core jobs (or not-so-cerebral jobs), multi-tasking would be easy. Unfortunately, that is not the case. In real life, businesses suffer from a lot of headaches (cerebral thinking), which restrain them from taking on new risks. And businesses, also, do not divide the strategic core competencies and non-core jobs well. However, if businesses have an assurance of a definitive outcome with regard to non-core jobs from engagement with subject matter experts that have specialized in those areas of enabling their customers, those businesses can focus on core problems better. As a result, those businesses can engage better with customers by educating and being educated by customers, by enabling customers and being enabled by the customers, effecting a change and thus engaging with the customers.

2

EDUCATE PHASE

The Mahabharata, one of the two great epics of ancient India, describes a great war between the Pandavas and Kauravas. While the Pandavas were a much weaker group, it also had a great strategist in their group in the form of Lord Krishna. Krishna became Prince Arjuna's charioteer and orchestrated the war against the Kauravas. Krishna taught Arjuna that the righteous path was not easy and that a man's duty lies in working toward a goal without worrying about the outcome (and letting God decide the results).

The Kauravas, on the other hand, had three great commanders: Bheesma, Drona, and Karna. Each commander was well-versed in the art of war and a supreme warrior adept at military strategies.

Lord Krishna was not a warrior himself. However, he had researched ways to manage the battles. He educated the Pandava brothers about the weaknesses of their opponents and designed elaborate plans around these competitive advantages. The strategies, which were formed subsequently, won the war for the Pandavas, even though their army was a fraction of what their opponent's had.

Whether the end goal be gaining military advantage or development or sale of a product, education is a key input to all game plans. Traditionally, marketing used to focus on outreach aspects and providing prospective customers high-level product information through education. And as a result, education has always been a major part of marketing initiatives, but as more and more new businesses are empowered by the Internet and globalization, the education aspect of marketing has taken on a much wider meaning. It is becoming more bidirectional and is tied closely to customer engagement.

The Education phase of the Four E framework is not only about educating prospective customers about features of a new product, it is also about educating the company team through researching customers, competitors and other sources to see if the entrepreneurial business or product is viable and sustainable. Education of the customer helps in establishing a platform and a loyal base of customers, and subsequently identifying what levers to use to make it grow.

Education also brings forth the strategic goals of the entrepreneur, or why he wants to be in this business in the first place. Is there a space where he thinks his solution will easily fit? Or is he passionate about some ideas and ready to do anything to get there?

***

Let us talk about Shah Rukh Khan—a superstar in Bollywood. What kind of background did he have before he became a star? Average or none? Did he know anyone influential in the industry? Probably not. Did everyone in India know him? Yes.

Perhaps the last response says it all. Bollywood (like Hollywood) used to be driven by influence and who you knew in the 1970s and 1980s. But things started changing in the early 1990s. It no longer mattered who you knew, but who knew you. Now take into consideration the power of social network, which is all about how networked you are—or how many people know you and how much do you influence them with your own stories?

The entertainment business is highly influenced by star power. The sons and daughters of stars also retain some of the power that their fathers or mothers brokered a generation ago. Needless to say, it is natural that they become successful as people have been following stories about them all along in film magazines and tabloids.

Shah Rukh did not have star power. He started as a TV actor just before the cable TV growth exploded in India. TV viewers had only so many channels to watch in those days. Shah Rukh became an overnight success with a series of TV shows in the late 1980s and the early 1990s and then he decided to act in movies. Translating the TV success into cinema success was not that easy, but it did help him cross the popularity chasm as TV built a platform for him. Everyone watching TV got educated about Shah Rukh.

Now let us take the case of *American Idol*. The same idea applies. The artist educates viewers on TV first and establishes that platform and helps their transition to another form of entertainment while also helping in sale of related merchandize like music CDs.

While we are still talking about show business and influencing CD sales, it is important to point out that movie trailers have traditionally done a great job of educating customers about movies, and building a platform quickly. In Indian movies, which are typically musicals, songs/dances play an even more important educating role than trailers and determining the success of movies. Songs compete in their own market.

The success of a song in the music market is tightly integrated with the success of a movie. It also acts as a promotional assist for the movie producers. In other words, the movie gets multiple chances to make it big with multiple channels of education.

***

A lot of entrepreneurs do not necessarily allocate enough resources for educating prospective customers or even existing customers. However, education forms an integral part of communicating the benefits of products or services. Again, entrepreneurial firms need not put all their eggs in the Educate basket. Remember, there are only so many dollars and you have to put them in the right Es. But firms with products or services that are complex and about which customers do not have much understanding (not even knowing how the services offered differ from a competing entity), must have a budget set aside for the Educate phase. The educators reach out to prospects, gather what customers need, inform them about the new products in the pipeline, and start observing what customers value.

Messaging through different media and conferences help spread the word around. The same touch points can help the entrepreneur to learn from prospective customers about their pain points. As education is a bidirectional effort, the users educate the educator about functions that are most valued by them so that the educators can then reach back to the users with new product functionalities. It is all about functionalities and values, after all.

Figure 2.2 Educate

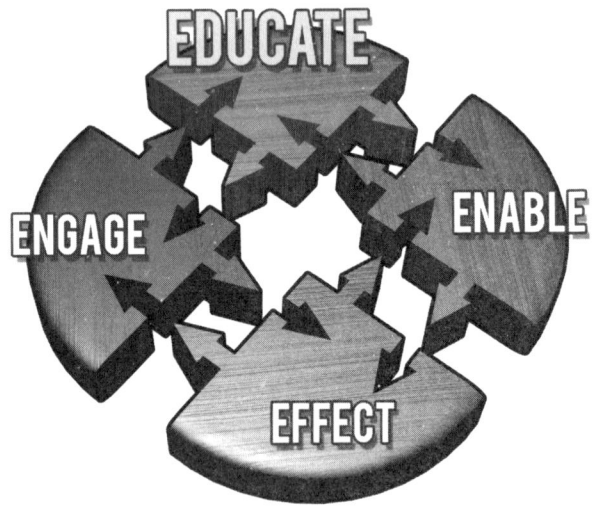

CONDUCT RESEARCH

Before you start educating the customer, think about educating yourself first. What do you know about the market? Who are those playing in the market? Will the big players or first movers always have an advantage over you?

The Educate phase helps get the entrepreneur up to speed on the customers and competitors. Educating, in other words, is about identifying the boundaries of what I call the engaging zone. The engaging zone is the zone where the entrepreneur and his customer are both creating value for each other. The educator wants to find out what the customers really value and thus designs the products per those findings. At times, this can be difficult as the customers' values keep changing or a large competitor may introduce a product similar to the entrepreneur's.

Sun Tzu, in his writings on the art of war, teaches the importance of recognizing strategic opportunities. He also explains how to react to changing circumstances

Figure 2.3 Questionnaire Sample

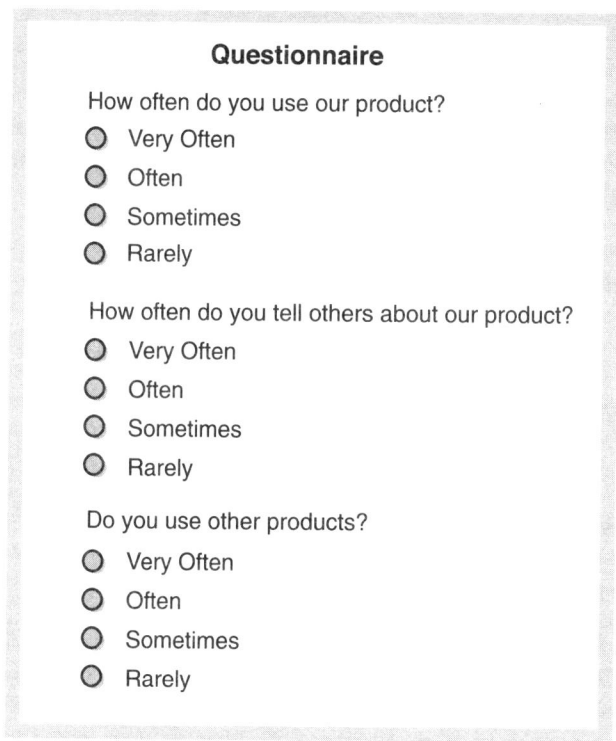

and advises that successful military campaigns are about limiting the cost of competing and the cost from subsequent damage. If your business is new, you have to come up with unconventional methods. Competing with bigger firms head-on is not the best way to be the frontrunner. A successful entrepreneur not only takes his enemies by surprise but also gives the illusion that his army is as big an army as the competitor's. This illusion these days can be implemented through effective and agile use of resources without being an extravagant spender in bells and whistles.

In addition, being smaller (and entrepreneurial) helps in exploring and researching, more than when running a large organization with several departments, each with its own marketing team and cost center. It is very difficult to maneuver such a large ship. Besides, larger and more established firms suffer from complacency. They have done quite a few things right, so working continuously towards groundbreaking research to do better dies away with size and day-to-day fire-fighting. When a disruptive technology or product appears, survival becomes the greatest challenge. Think about Kodak, which went through such an ordeal when digital cameras came into the market.

RESEARCH WHERE?

Being agile and alert is an important aspect of the educator's job. To identify trends and opportunities, educators should constantly scan and gather information on events occurring in the market or at other competing firms. The educators should identify trends in demographics, socio-cultural groups, economics, regulations, competition, and new technologies. Threats and opportunities can stem from various sources and so scanning helps entrepreneurs identify issues in the market. Entrepreneurs can run statistical algorithms (chi-squared tests, linear regression, multi-variate analyses, and binomial distributions) to identify trends from the data. However, interpreting the dynamically changing market is more than just data interpretation and needs a deeper insight into the problems of customers to understand how the evolving products could focus on the engaging zone and make the problems go away.

The typical market environment is a combination of micro environment (forces internal to the firm at play), meso environment (members of the industry at play) and macro environment (larger forces, beyond the market, such as regulations and new technology). Research can be conducted on the macro and meso environments first to get the big-picture viability of a product. Subsequently, field and desk research should be conducted to gather and analyze more data on the micro environment.

VALUE AND NEEDS

Bread for one person can be wine for another. We all have different value systems—due to our socio-cultural backgrounds, and habits we have acquired from places of education and work. We have also learned from influencers and peers that inspire us, and because of different psycho-physiological conditions while growing up and multiple other media sources such as from people, TV programs and magazines.

That value system also helps us develop needs and wants, and assign value to these needs (and also to the solutions that fulfill these needs). The identification of value helps entrepreneurs in building product functionalities.

Based on that value system, consumers also develop a "willingness to pay" range for these product functionalities. For example, my willingness to pay for a burger is $3–$4 if I have to buy from a quick service restaurant or up to $10, if I go to a gourmet burger place. My best friend has a different range of willingness to pay for the same food.

The educator identifies this willingness to pay for product functions and then works with the enabler and effecter to raise this willingness to pay higher by convincing the customer that the value the product brings is more than what the customer perceives. For example, some burger companies advertise how fresh their ingredients are and they convince the customer that it is okay to pay premium for that freshness.

Now, is that really so difficult? In a vast majority of the companies that I have come across, it could be true. The marketing team does not even know what the real customer needs are, let alone having a unanimous understanding as to which of those needs are to be priced a notch higher.

Can an entrepreneur satisfy customer needs when he does not know what they are? Often entrepreneurs like to think they have a blockbuster product and everyone will buy that. And when it does not happen the way the entrepreneur had forecast, he shifts the blame onto the customers. The entrepreneur likes to think that customers have needs they do not even know they have and that they will want the product after they see it. The entrepreneur also believes that customers cannot articulate their needs; and that their priorities change unreasonably all the time.

As innovating entrepreneurs center their efforts on their specialties and earlier products they have built (after their research), they may not see what kind of value they are developing by building a solution, and thus may completely miss the actual problem. And they are not wrong most of the time, but the fact that entrepreneurs love their solutions too much and bet everything on the product is as much a point to be factored in during product development as consumers changing what they value from time to time. Perhaps that is why Henry Ford had said, "If I had asked people what they wanted, they would have said faster horses".

SO, WHAT IS "VALUE" AGAIN?

Before we go any further, it may be a good idea to catch up on what exactly brings value to the customer.

What would the customer pay for consuming that product or what would a customer sacrifice to buy the product in question, and why? How would the customer want the product delivered—and how often? Will any kind of bundling help the customer make the decision? Will a product's packaging appeal to the target customer?

If we look at some of the leading innovations of this age, we will notice how they added value not only by offering solutions for pains, but also were affordable, accessible and timed appropriately for introducing value.

At ABC Engineering, the department that identified the pain also collected information on what customers valued around price, important functions, and durability. Accordingly, the educators recorded the "value" areas for these customers. Subsequently, they established the value proposition as a compelling message around solving the primary problem within a specific period of time and using actionable metrics.

THE CASE OF RENTING VIDEOS BY MAIL (NETFLIX)

Overdue fines of $40 are what led Reed Hastings to start Netflix. Its web launch took place in 1997. The monthly subscription concept evolved incrementally, and was initiated by Netflix in September 1999. Netflix built its reputation on a new business model of flat-fee unlimited rentals without due dates, late fees, or shipping and handling fees. Subscription fee was not a new concept; it existed for consumers of rental facilities, utilities, newspapers, and gymnasiums. This was, however, new for the home entertainment market. And, so for Netflix, it required a solid understanding of the market need (or in essence what customers valued).

Netflix's depth of movie offerings, and other online features such as reviews, makes it appealing across the board. Unlike a brick and mortar video rental store, which makes money from the recent titles, Netflix's revenue comes from a much broader selection, which it streams and sends out every day.

Source: http://www.economist.com/node/4149765 (Accessed on November 3, 2015).

Netflix posted its first profit (over $6 million) in 2003. In 2005, Netflix reached another milestone—it had started shipping a million DVDs out every day. Netflix continued its evolutionary path, and in 2007 its journey saw it going into the video-on-demand market. As a result, even though DVD sales went down after 2006, Netflix grew.

Let us quickly summarize this situation. Pain Points: Late fees were always a pain; the single rental pricing had become exorbitant.

Value Added: A subscription service would not necessitate going to a shop to return videos/DVDs; an Internet store offered a much broader choice list; the subscription service/video streaming was priced reasonably; no late fees; e-commerce and shipping were widely used

The value proposition considered unmet needs such as no late fees, timely delivery by mail, a great spread of videos to choose from and a low price. As video subscription through mail was still a novel concept, it took the company quite some time and effort to get the message out there to the prospects, educate them and cross the chasm. The prospects soon realized the value that came with Netflix's service.

Netflix claimed that, with the aid of a browser applet, customers could start playing the movies within 15 seconds of clicking the button—compare that with going to a store and picking a movie and then putting it in a DVD player.

Source: http://arstechnica.com/uncategorized/2007/01/ 8627/ (Accessed on November 3, 2015).

A customer value proposition is a clear, concise and compelling articulation of how the factors that are important to the customer are served by the product. A product with a strong value proposition is directly linked to its performance and price (as compared to that of the competition), and must offer value through price or differentiation (quality, more functionalities, etc.) in order to be successful. A good customer value proposition convinces the customers why the product is different from other products, and also why they should buy the product.

The proposition should also focus on only the few attributes (or even the single most important attribute) important to the customer to bring forth the value these differences bring, and then communicate this in a very compelling, clear and concise way. A brand takes the value proposition a step further, and it cements this usefulness as an image in the minds of consumers.

WHO SHOULD YOU DISPLEASE?

Great companies are not good at everything. The entrepreneurs should understand their strengths well but their weaknesses even better. To stay competitive, they certainly

Figure 2.4 Value Proposition

Things to consider while designing your value proposition

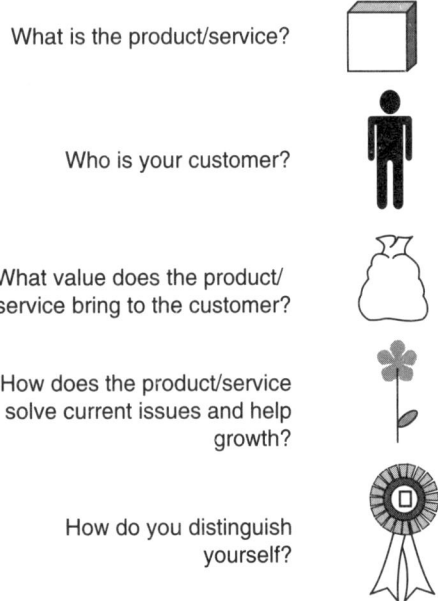

What is the product/service?

Who is your customer?

What value does the product/service bring to the customer?

How does the product/service solve current issues and help growth?

How do you distinguish yourself?

have to consider some cost saving in areas not held high on their customers' priorities. This is very similar to how you would respond to the question you may be asked in a job interview: "What are your weak areas?"

Walmart's minimal stress on experiential selling, for instance, serves its loyal customers well, with mindsets that they will find less of an experiential wow when they get in the store. Walmart's customers do not expect the store to build on that aspect going forward, either, as it is less of a priority for Walmart.

For entrepreneurs, it makes more sense to cater to some segments only and not try to please all segments all the time. Before Suzanne started her Middle Eastern restaurant, she had toyed with the idea of opening a multi-ethnic cuisine restaurant in the heart of the city. When she conducted her due diligence in the same location, she identified that she would not get the critical mass, and it would be a long time before she could get multiple ethnicities to visit her restaurant. By then, the high burn-out rate would have eaten her business.

MARKET SUITABILITY AND ADAPTABILITY

Customers change with time either because (a) an evolving product's target segment changes to include new customers, and/or; (b) existing customers have new preferences and values. Let us take a typical workplace as an example. The workplace now has a lot of single career women over 28 years old. The workplace also includes people from all around the globe, speaking different languages and thinking differently. What was important two decades ago may not be as important now. Having a prestigious job may not be as important as holding valuable assets with a stable cash flow under your name. At the same time, passion and working in a cerebral function is now more important than getting paid more for doing a high-paying, monkey job. In other words, the culture is changing, and with that, the values of the marketplace are transforming too.

While value introduction is a key to educating customers, the state of the market and environment suitability play an equally important role. What would have happened if Netflix had started back in the 1970s or 1980s? Would it have been viable? Perhaps not (at least not with the same business model).

More importantly, Netflix started because video stores existed that were renting video cassettes and DVDs in the first place, and so the idea of renting movies was already there. The environment, the openness of the customers to use such a service, and the existing trends in the industry all added to the suitability and growth of the product.

Incremental evolution is equally important. Netflix completely stopped the single video rental once it found that flat-fee subscription was the new trend. Apart from a deep understanding of the market, such a transition requires the entrepreneur to gauge what competing services and complementing industries are doing to cater to the ever-changing customer priorities.

The iPod brought Apple back from a possible bankruptcy in 1997. Not only that, it also became a bestselling product. But the iPod alone would not have sustained Apple as the market had other gadgets that stored music and were also used for additional functions. That is when the iPhone came into the picture. So, why did the iPod and iPhone succeed while others did not? Apple evolved (or pivoted) incrementally, and made its product increasingly better to educate and engage customers. In retrospect, Apple could have been obliterated if this shift in business focus had not happened.

Adapting has to be done right. Wrong choices in adapting would also set a firm on the path of obliteration, in the same way as making no choice. If you look at BlackBerry, you will see that perhaps the company had ideas, but did not make the right choices, and as a result iPhone and Android phones ate big portions of BlackBerry's market share.

If a company cannot adapt, it does not survive. Steve Jobs, after coming back into Apple, built the company back up. The iPod turned into a huge product line. Jobs also identified that he should focus on designing a phone as new phones would be able to store just as much music, and had to pivot.

Source: http://www.theguardian.com/commentisfree/ 2013/nov/05/why-blackberry-failed (Accessed on November 3, 2015).

DRIVE AND STRATEGIC PERSPECTIVE

Perhaps a lot of entrepreneurs did not have a clear goal as to what they wanted to do, and also had no access to market research numbers from earlier days, but as data got collected and analyzed, entrepreneurs started getting a grip on how things ultimately work out.

During his travels, Blake Mycoskie had observed some of the hardships faced by children. Mycoskie was particularly pained too see those who did not have shoes. He wanted to create a sustainable cause-related business, where it could provide articles to people in need. Mycoskie took that idea further and conceived the business model for TOMS to provide a child in need a pair of shoes with each pair purchased, which he called the "one for one" model. Subsequently, he applied the same model to other products. Mycoskie's drive and the evolution of his strategy helped him in building the model and in the fulfillment of his vision and other ideas downstream.

Blake Mycoskie started five businesses, his first one was a successful campus laundry service that he sold later. He wanted to create a business not reliant on donations, and that provided the powerful foundation for TOMS.

Source: http://www.toms.com/blakes-bio (Accessed on November 3, 2015).

For the entrepreneur, education takes place the best with products that can be tailored to customer feedback. The entrepreneur gets to interact with customer groups, listen to discover new functionalities, and tweak his own plans. Along with that, a periodic outreach to customers by an entrepreneur makes the customers aware of any new products/ services that were added to the entrepreneur's catalog.

PRODUCT DESIGN

Along with a well-articulated business strategy, the entrepreneur should regularly visit the product design. This has to be done based on customer inputs gathered by the educator team and from the feedback the educators receive from enablers, effecters, and engagers. The objective is to study the connection between product, the end user, and the environment. The entrepreneur should consult with industrial and concept design experts and see how to evolve the minimum viable product economically (to reach the MVP) and get customers addicted to it.

Industrial design helps visualize how the product will look and appeal to the end user, with a focus on ergonomic appeal, aesthetic appeal, and the human factor (how it will best be used by the consumer).

The actual engineering design is the next design step to fully develop the product into a functional and

Figure 2.5 Product Design

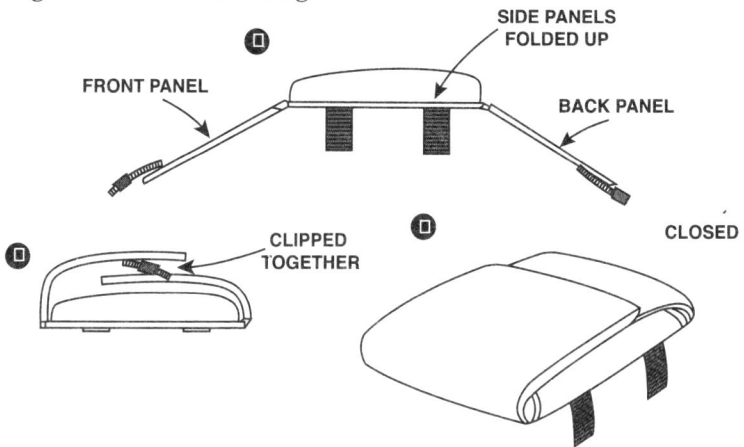

manufactured product in the most optimum way. The design evolves with the phases. It starts with what we know from the researched data in the Education component and as we move into the Enabling component, we look how to produce a product inexpensively, or distribute it effectively, among other things. *Effect* is when we complete product development (the customer accepts the product and buys it), and we are satisfied that it solves customer problems. Thus, ensuring we get the customer into the engaging zone. *Engage* ensures that the customer buys into any new functionalities offered and remains engaged. Subsequent to that, the customer shares feedback, after using the product, with the entrepreneur and educates him about ways to improve the product—thus starting the cycle of Four E again.

AVOIDING "WTF JUST HAPPENED" MOMENTS

Entrepreneurs who do not take into consideration both negative and positive outcomes seem to be not prepared for major changes. A lot of entrepreneurs follow their hearts while running the business. They are successful in the market for a while, and then keep repeating what they started without evolving their products or styles. They just hope that the flow of cash remains unabated. They often unreasonably allow the status quo to continue for years and then see the business trends change on them.

After not following the news for a little while, they take heed of what analysts are saying about their industries. They are appalled when they notice that alternative products are market leaders. To the entrepreneur, this is also referred to as a "WTF just happened" moment.

This is somewhat comparable to the ordeals of BlackBerry and Kodak, both of which were leading markets until the wind simply changed direction. Perhaps they should have revisited their strategic goals and designs more often. Let us take the case of some of these products that may possibly see a vanishing demand or which may see a WTF just happened moment soon.

VCRs went out of business after DVDs came out, and now DVDs/Blu-ray discs may experience the same plight as video streaming becomes the favorite, thanks to the efforts of Netflix, Hulu, Amazon, YouTube, Vudu, and others. With GPS mapping now being a part of smartphone services, GPS units for vehicles are no more an unmet need. With high-quality resolution cameras in smartphones on the rise, the camera lines, too, will encounter their death soon.

In his blog, Micah Singleton points out, with valid reasons, why 5 different products will be less needed by consumers—these 5 products are a) Blue Ray/DVD players, b) GPS units in cars, c) dial up internet (which I think is already extinct), d) low-end digital cameras (some

(Continued)

people have still been holding onto them for memory's sake) and e) car keys (I think it may take some time to get out of car keys).

Source: http://www.techlicious.com/blog/5-tech-products-that-will-be-dead-in-5-years-2013/ (Accessed on November 3, 2015).

KEEP CUSTOMERS INFORMED AND LOYAL

Many entrepreneurs do what their passion tells them, and so they elaborate on the features and benefits of their products and services. They often make wrong assumptions about the problems, and pains their customers have and talk how their product could solve those.

Educating the customer on all possible issues and informing them about all potential solutions builds trust with the customer. Apple introduced its tablet product features one by one, and by doing that, it educated its customers to understand the various product functionalities. Facebook, as we saw earlier, had customers sit with educators.

Businesses don't take the time to rethink if their messaging is aligned with what the clients need to hear. Businesses wrongly believe that education of consumers has to do with elaborating upon the features and functionalities of their product, and not how the product can solve a problem for consumers. And so with the assumption that prospects already have all the necessary facts, and are deciding between brands, they ignore the fact that the

(Continued)

(*Continued*)

> prospect may not even know what problem the product solves. Had the business educated the prospect on the problem and all possible solutions, the business would have built the trust of the prospect.
>
> *Source:* http://www.businessinsider.com/how-brands-can-educate-customers-2013-4#ixzz2oR57J6Ws (Accessed on November 3, 2015).

A vast number of entrepreneurial firms, however, are not eager to invest in educating customers as they do not appreciate any clear benefit in doing so. A recent study published in the MIT Sloan Management Review shows how education helps not so much with the content but with trust. A survey was conducted across 1,200 retail clients of a financial services' company in Melbourne, Australia. The study showed that initiatives to enhance prospects' overall understanding had a positive and strong impact on building trust. The more customers know from you about all the options and the field in general, the more loyal they become to good service.

> The complete study is contained in "Perceived Service Quality and Customer Trust: Does Enhancing Customers' Service Knowledge Matter?" The paper was published in the February 2008 issue of the Journal of Service Research.
>
> *Source:* http://sloanreview.mit.edu/article/customer-education-increases-trust/ (Accessed on November 3, 2015).

In essence, if someone takes the time to help you learn more about a subject, and gives a fair look at all the different options available, you will be more likely to return to that source of information again.

Talking about your product is good, but customers want to understand the field and the players in the field. Customers want to know about alternatives, and if this field may even provide the right solution.

Source: http://www.smallbizclub.com/component/k2/item/386-educate-your-customers (Accessed on November 3, 2015).

HOW EDUCATORS CAN INFLUENCE THE PROSPECT'S BRAIN AND WHAT PART

Since neuroscience opened the brain to marketers' scrutiny, it has been clear how we can influence the customer. Humans have three parts to our brains: the neocortex (the largest part of the cerebral cortex) that can work with complex thoughts, the limbic system that controls emotion and the stem that focuses on a more fundamental function—survival.

In educating existing customers, we have to target the lower two aspects of the brain, the limbic system (emotion) and the stem (survival), for closing the sale. On the other hand, if you are building a new product, the neocortex (complex thoughts) is what needs to be focused on to get customers engaged early on, along with the stem (survival).

So, let us see some examples as to which brain function will handle these situations for you:

1. You have a close friend and he is recommending a product—limbic
2. You are an employee and might be let go if you do not meet the target—stem
3. You are a manager, and a sales representative's talk about how his products' web version solves your problem—neocortex
4. You are stopped by a police officer, and if he talks to you for more than five minutes you will miss a meeting—stem
5. A team member explains his complex idea—neocortex
6. A team member fire-fights and saves the project—stem
7. A sales representative leaving a sticky point—limbic
8. You have seen a logo or visual that you like—limbic
9. You remember a visual that you had a good experience with—limbic
10. You went inside a restaurant where you did not like the food quality—neocortex
11. Your friend recommended a restaurant and you happened to pass by it—limbic
12. You go to a drug store, and you remember that the drug you want to buy can cause an increase in heart rate—Stem

You may have noticed one trend clearly—brand and repeat buying is quite a lot about emotions. A lot of entrepreneurial marketers target the limbic system by anchoring with something that the prospects already favor. The marketers, who work in compliance areas, use the stem

Figure 2.6 The Human Brain

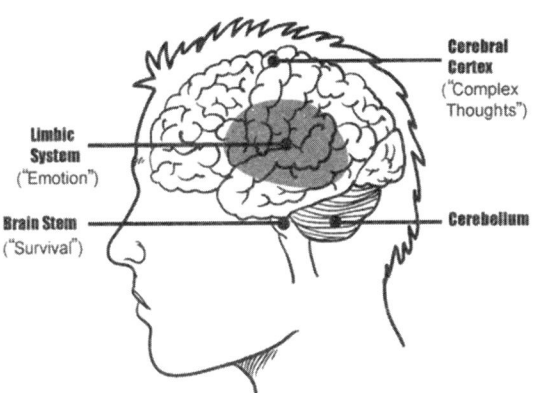

while referring to the regulatory stick and let their customers know the consequences if they are not compliant.

- The Stem—The brain stem (also referred to as "reptilian"), deals with survival and instinctive functions. It is responsible for tasks required for self-preservation.
- The Limbic System—The limbic system adds feelings to basic preservation functions.
- The neocortex—The neocortex provides reason and logic.

Source: http://www.ascd.org/publications/books/101269/chapters/A-Walk-Through-the-Brain.aspx; And http://thinkbynumbers.org/statistical-cost-benefit-analysis-vs-irrational-emotion/ (Accessed on November 3, 2015).

The initial interaction happens in the education phase, but the next few phases make this engagement stronger.

In the next chapters, we will talk about enabling, effecting, and engaging a customer.

EDUCATOR CHARACTERISTICS

Existing products in the market play an important role. Besides the educational activities of the entrepreneur, their interaction skills play a critical role as well.

So what skills are important for a top educator? At ABC Engineering, they hired a lot of their educators, who were:

- Empathizing—Empathy is the skill of imagining oneself in any other person's position, and subsequently understanding what his/her unmet needs and values are. Empathizing helps the educator read the prospect's mind and educate that person in the areas he/she needs more information on.
- Interpersonal—What is empathy without interpersonal skills in educating? Hence, it becomes very important to have skills to connect with others easily, listen to them, and help them share their needs/pains.
- Communicative—Communication skills, as in persuasive written and oral abilities, are very important to convey the message to the team as well as elicit information from prospects.
- Strong at analytics—Analytical skills pertain to extracting conclusions from data for making decisions.
- Exposed to different cultures—Identifying what customers value, what virtues they are exposed to and what is shaping their priorities becomes easy if the educator has had a broad cultural exposure.

CHAPTER SUMMARY

The Educate Phase gave us tools for understanding the needs of the customers, as well as reaching out to prospective customers and informing them about new products. This bidirectional interaction sets the tone and cadence for the engaging zone, at large, between the entrepreneur and the customer.

It starts with conducting research to identify potential customers. This can be done by observing the trends in the industry through statistical analysis as well as by building competitive intelligence to identify strategic opportunities in the market.

Identification of pain points and real needs can help an entrepreneur in setting a benchmark price for a solution. Knowing the value is important, as you do not want your product to be priced out of market neither do you want it to be so inexpensive that customers just do not get it. However, in order to even build the product there has to be a true market for it—and so the entrepreneur needs to refine that aspect.

In going through these iterations, we saw how the drive and the strategic vision of the entrepreneur helped the product through evolution stages. With each incremental evolution came a new design better suited to meet customer needs, or one that could be produced more economically. Before we do a design-and-build overkill, checking with the customer and keeping him informed about the changes is sensible. It is worthwhile to even find out whether people want a new functionality on the existing product and are willing to pay that extra buck to get that project underway.

The Educate phase also talked about some of the skills that help teams that are educating. Skills around

Figure 2.7 Your Music Band

empathy, communication, and analysis help the educators immensely. The next chapter on the Enable phase takes what you have learned during Educate and builds on that. There you enable yourself, the product, and also your customers by making the product affordable and accessible. In other words, you bring the customers into an engaging zone that works for you, the entrepreneur.

Case Study—Your Music Band, Inc.

Let us consider you have a music band (in other words you have friends that play in your garage). You want it to succeed and you do not have a lot of funds. How would you start educating, and be well set on a path to becoming popular?

So, you start singing popular album cover songs and you research through the customer reactions (e.g., they become very excited when you sing some heavy metal numbers). You come to the conclusion that you should specialize in that area that the audience loves.

You start playing at various festivals and events to earn money and are able to better gauge what brings value to the audience. You decide if the market is ready for your style. If not, what style does the market want? You recruit a dedicated guitarist so that you can focus more on the vocal aspect, which is your forte, and craft your uniqueness for your audience. You identify people who are ready to become your loyal audience so that you can build a platform.

Now you are getting busy in writing songs, composing tunes, and testing them with your loyal group. Perhaps you get a two thumbs up with one or more of your songs. You post them on YouTube but they do not go viral. But, you have recording firms, and event managers calling you. What should you do at this point?

You bump into a friend, who talks about the success he saw in selling his idea on a website. Shortly thereafter, you hire a web team to develop your online presence and educate more people about your group. But you are burning your saved money every day. Your loyal customers are not necessarily buying anything from you. They come where you sing but you have not made a lot in sales. Is it time to assess the market for a product or service that you

(Continued)

(*Continued*)

can monetize? Do you fear that asking them to pay to hear your songs may make them never come back?

Sometimes, even gathering a good platform is seen as a potential for making money and cascading sales—so you are not on the wrong path. Your loyal customers certainly are spending their time with you and time is money. Do you plan to have some way to communicate to them about your future plans such as which locations will you be singing at, and if you are offering discounts and promotions to early birds and so on.

As you are working with the emotional side of your customer base, a lot of your messaging has to be around the limbic system. What kind of outreach would you plan for in that case?

Some of these answers will be better answered in the next few chapters but the education aspect will set the tone of your relationship and interactions with your customers and will help you look for engaging opportunities all the time.

3

ENABLE PHASE

The education of the Pandavas on the weaknesses of the Kaurava commanders guided them to win the war against the Kauravas. With limited resources but key information at their disposal, the Pandavas planned their execution in an optimum manner. If that had not been done, the Pandavas would have lost the war. We saw during the Educate phase that an entrepreneur gathers information about the need, conceptualizes the design as per the need of the market, and then disseminates key details about that information. Questions concerning market feasibility are answered with the help of research.

The Enable phase takes the research and dissemination process a notch higher and puts emphasis on execution as per what was understood about the customer—what he likes, where he goes for shopping, how much is his willingness to pay for a particular product, what promotion excites him, how he accesses information about a product, and how he eventually buys a product and consumes it.

Loosely speaking, in this phase, the entrepreneur gets enabled by considering product functions that customers need. Then he enables the customers by playing with the price, product, promotion, place, and other levers.

Entrepreneurs do a few things well in understanding the needs of their customers. However, not all of them examine the host of other questions, and only a few strategically shape their offerings. Enabling is about understanding the customers intricately so as to build a solution that fits customer needs better than other solutions out there.

The Educate phase is important for companies with groundbreaking innovations or completely new solutions, as the product viability is still being tested in those cases. The Enable function is more pronounced for products that have already been proven viable, but where the entrepreneur needs to increase the reach and better serve customers. Solid enabling processes help customers realize the benefits the product offers.

Enabling is essentially a series of activities in which users are analyzed to identify the areas that are most lucrative, the segments that value the product the most, and the product functionalities that are most sought after. And for that, the marketing department reaches

Figure 3.1 Enable

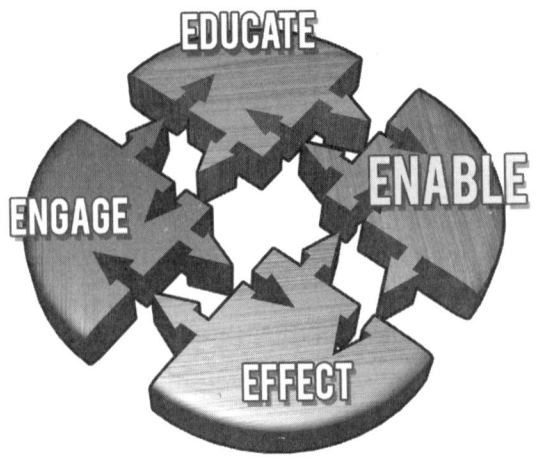

out to prospects and customers and surveys their interests to inquire why they buy, what they buy, when do they buy, and how community influences them.

The key for the entrepreneur is to interpret all this data and take action to reach out better, bring the customers into an engaging zone that works for the entrepreneur and subsequently make customers loyal—thus maximizing profits and strengthening the brand.

KNOWING YOUR CUSTOMER

The Figaro marketing team knew the buying preferences of its prospects. They knew a lot about their customers—their demographic particulars, what they valued and what their interests were. When a new management team started at Figaro X-ray, the marketing team was asked to spend time with orthopedic and dental technicians and shadow these technicians for a day and discover how the immobility of their patients determined their schedule. Through that, they took an inventory of all functionalities that would help the technicians. The marketers also reached out to prospects through social media, and recorded the popular trends.

Companies such as Figaro that strive constantly to know their customers intimately use this information to their competitive advantage. They enable their customers and get them the service in the best possible way. If they do not do that, they will miss opportunities and eventually lose the customer to competition.

What happened to Kodak, the strong 120-year-old firm that had popularized film and camera products? We can see a theme of missed openings and lost opportunities. It seems management did not gauge how the image world would change with the advent of digital images. Perhaps the company never was close with their customers to understand their changing priorities. Kodak remained under the impression that its customers would stick to the traditional film and camera lines, and hence never paid too much attention to the digital line of business. Kodak forgot that customers bought solutions to their problems and not just the product.

There is an article that talks about missed opportunities by Kodak. With the arrival of digital images and digital cameras, Kodak stayed with its traditional business lines—never foreseeing that even loyal customers leave if they find better value in other products.

Source: http://www.forbes.com/sites/alanhall/2012/06/14/to-succeed-as-an-entrepreneur-know-your-customer/#28048214755e) (Accessed on May 23, 2016).

WHAT CUSTOMERS DO NOT LIKE

Customers told Kabob Times several times that they wanted their pita breads to be made out of multi-grain and not plain wheat. Suzanne Poupolis of Kabob Times was also told by customers that in order to make customers come back she should have had more parking spots. She also received numerous suggestions about other food items. The comments from customers provided a great opportunity for creating new menu items, opening a branch shop at another location with more parking, and expanding the business in various ways.

Figaro had implemented web analytics to find information on websites used by visitors and the search terms these visitors had used. The site visitor locations identified the geographies where their marketing focus should be, while the search terms gave information about what these prospects were looking for. Figaro also regularly looked at the comments and complaints that were posted on various websites.

The company noticed that a vast majority of issues were part of a few broad categories. The issue owners then looked at the root causes, resolved the issues, attended to the voice of the customer and all factors critical to quality, and recorded the solution. This whole process created their first ever issue log, which expedited future issue identification and resolution, and brought about a formal knowledge management system.

The company also identified that among the wasteful activities, the worst one was to talk to customers about products that the customers did not need. Figaro had segmented customers. It served the high ROI segments with more resources and spent less (or no) time for segments that had low returns. Figaro also analyzed the top customers, and identified ways to keep them satisfied and make them evangelists of Figaro's.

DATA, DATA EVERYWHERE, BUT IS IT ALL USABLE?

Figaro conducted several internal workshops and after noticing that the data scientists were defining all steps and not letting others be a part of the sharing process, they wanted to make it an open forum. They wanted everyone to contribute to the learning aspect. In fact, they started observing certain procedures so that:

1. The team members stay unbiased and allow the data to speak for itself.
2. They did not let any data fall through the cracks to ensure they get a full view of customers.
3. They captured all sorts of data, particularly the outliers and granular level data.
4. They incorporated continuously changing requirements that they obtained from the data.
5. They captured experiences from data from various devices and applications.

Predictive analytics and other data analyses (such as cohort analysis) use data from the past and predict what could happen in the future, which helps in planning and decision making. Organizations such as Figaro should not wait till issues snowball to make critical choices. A pro-active approach of carefully observing the trends so that there are actionable check points and not just a hindsight perspective helps enabling.

Models that provide intelligence to solve issues, or give input to strategic goals, are very important for the enabler. As the data is so extensive, the entrepreneur always needs to scan, and massage the data to extract the best possible information. A well-trained model should be of value right away. Again, too much dependence on predictive analytics is as bad as too little dependence. So, plans to use that as an important input should be defined at the outset. The entrepreneur should also ensure that the predictive model is adopted as soon as it is implemented as it will not only enable customers, but also re-engage those who are not fully engaged, and educate those who have no (or only some) idea about the products.

***

Forecasting using data analysis is not new. Weather forecasting has been around for a long time. Weathermen analyze a mix of historical data, and existing conditions to derive a picture for the future. Similarly, data analysis has been used widely for medical/healthcare innovations for treating patients and identifying cures.

When John Katz, the salesman in the contingency business, took data samples from his prospective customers, he ran a bunch of rules and showed his prospects how much they could save. He built a system with data from the past and figured out the areas that needed more attention. His advantage was the strong data analytics group that he worked with who churned data for key information.

Figure 3.2 Lead Qualification Process

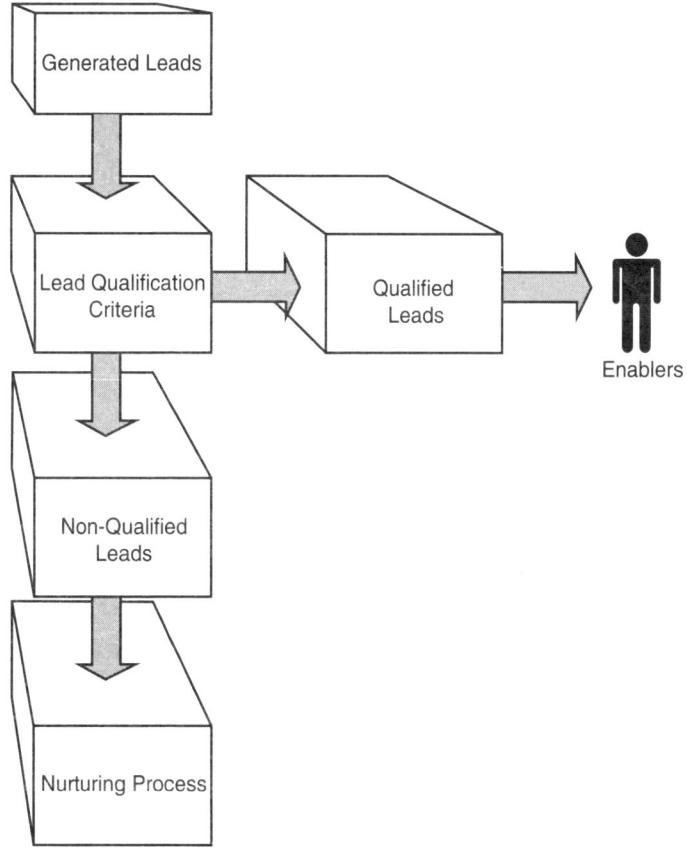

LEAD QUALIFICATION AND CRM

Figaro X-ray had a list of leads from the data that it collected from a cold calling program it had started a few years before. That led to a contact management system at Figaro. They kept adding more data items on the follow-ups, and hours spent, among other details. Later, they called it their customer relationship management (CRM) system.

The idea was to generate leads from various places including Figaro's website, presentations, surveys, tradeshows, and lists of companies that used other x-ray products. Then, they recorded information about clinics that were planning to expand services, and get into diagnostics, osteopathic and orthopedics. Those leads were primarily generated from the Educate phase. The plan during the Enable phase was to categorize these leads into suspects (if these leads had possible needs in the long term) or prospects (if the need was immediate). If the leads did not meet the qualification criteria they were set aside for further nurturing, and passed back to Educators.

CATEGORIZING CUSTOMERS

Entrepreneurs have always sought to answer some fundamental questions: Who are my customers? What do they do? What are they exposed to, and how can I reach them?

With a limited amount of resources, picking right battles is the only way to sustain the business. Segmentation helps resource allocation by grouping customers with similar traits and behaviors and answering the aforementioned questions by analyzing relevant survey data. Entrepreneurs then focus on the segments that offer the maximum returns and customize their services and products to the needs of these segments.

Demographic segmentation is the most common method of categorizing customers. This segmentation deals with age, income, and gender among other basic factors. Geographic segmentation divides the target customers based on factors such as nations, regions, cities, and so on. Psychographic segmentation divides the customers according to their values and lifestyle. Besides these three, there are other segmentation methods that can be used as well, but these are the most popular ones.

Kabob Times, after getting its franchising plan together, started looking at the different segments that they catered to. In that process, they not only considered who the customers were but also tracked how they lived. Were they listening to Middle Eastern music and participating in cultural events? Did they eat out only if they could avail themselves of discounts? Did they tell everyone on social sites what they ate, and where they went?

This made the job of communicating and running promotions much easier for Kabob Times. Based on the data they gathered, the segments that favored them clearly stood out. Accordingly, they redesigned (and it was an iterative evolution) their menu to cater to these segments. They removed those items that had not been frequently ordered and focused on those items that had been ordered over and over. They could clearly see how this segmentation helped them focus their resources optimally.

ENABLING THROUGH PRICING

Pricing is the most important enabler. With some basic understanding of identifying customers and tracking their behaviors, Suzanne looked at the price.

Pricing is set in various ways—but the four most prevalent ones are:

Value-based pricing—This is based on the value that a customer attributes to a product/service. It is determined by the willingness of the customer to pay for a product. Customer surveys and workshops are conducted in order to get a good understanding of the value that the customer attaches to the solution. Purchase intent, win/loss analysis and financial value measurement are examples of basic research methods for identifying this value. The price that comes out as a result, enables the product to solve the problem.

Cost-based pricing—Cost is what determines the price for commodities, where the differentiation between competing products is negligible. The cheaper that you can buy the raw materials for, the lower your selling price for the finished products will be.

Salesman's pricing—This is a price that the salesman offers, when he decides to effect the sale, which is generally based on careful calculations by him. If his gut tells him he will lose a prospective customer by going below a certain price point, he will offer that price to bag the business. The salesman also does not want to lose much on the margin. Therefore, he is careful before he advances any discount.

Market-inspired pricing—In this type of pricing, the price of a product is based on what other players making competing, or complementing products are doing. This is where predatory pricing, limit pricing, and other pricing models (e.g., Freemium model and franchising set prices) come into play.

For most entrepreneurs, value-based pricing, market-inspired pricing, and cost-based pricing are the most important pricing methods for enabling their customers to buy the product.

Value-based pricing starts from understanding the pain and hence requires a careful assessment of how much a customer is willing to spend to reduce or offset the pain. Besides pain remediation, some of the value added is from what we call feel-good or emotional factors—such as consuming premium and better quality products (take the case of Evian or Whole Foods Market), among others.

Figaro arrived at a value-based price for every new product it launched—using the reference price (the price of the old/existing solution), revenue increase (increase in revenues for the customers from the use of the new product), and cost savings (reduction in customer costs from the use of new product). Figaro chose that route as its CEO had known about a client of his—a pharmaceutical company that used value-based pricing techniques to charge a higher price, and used studies to prove that the new drug could help patients avoid expensive surgery and thus save costs even at a higher drug price.

Before Kabob Times introduced a chain of Indian dishes, Suzanne, the owner had surveyed other local Indian restaurant-goers. It also meant getting inputs from existing customers on the menu items they liked and the price ballpark they were comfortable with. As a result, they added 10 new items and priced them per the value they carried for enabling the existing (and prospective) customers to order Indian food there.

With food, the value is less dependent on a pain or an unmet need. It is more of an emotional value. Emotion can motivate you to buy and use known (or popular) products. So if you go to a foreign country, you will probably eat at a chain restaurant known to you for its foods and prices. You feel safe about dining there.

That is where franchising helps. Franchises have standard pricing and uniform quality across their franchisees, which enable customers, who have already completed

Figure 3.3 Value-based Pricing

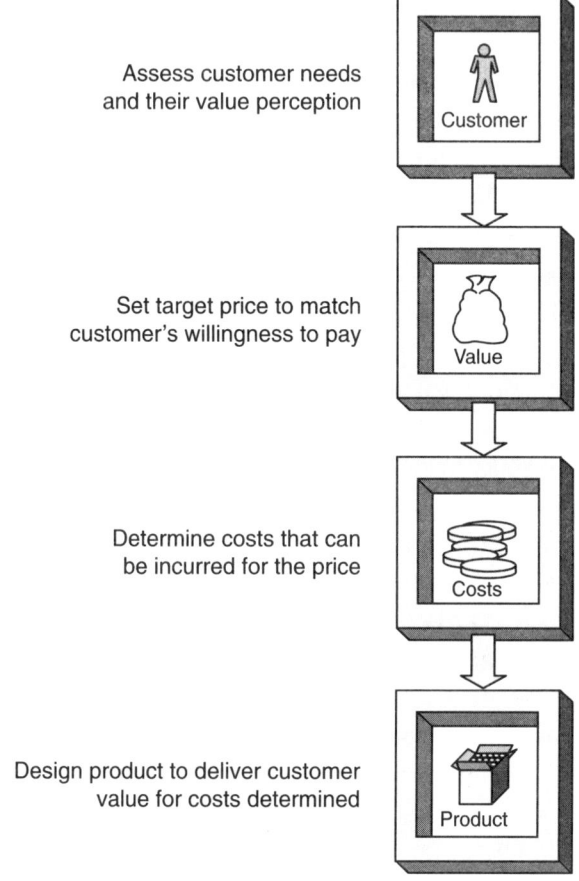

Assess customer needs and their value perception — Customer

Set target price to match customer's willingness to pay — Value

Determine costs that can be incurred for the price — Costs

Design product to deliver customer value for costs determined — Product

assessment of the value of the product. The purchase decision in such cases is easy. Hence, the attractiveness of franchising.

The other recent trend is try-and-buy or perhaps a little more elongated trial as in the freemium model (a market inspired pricing), intended to thwart the other players in the market. The users there pay for the product/services they get in a tiered sort of way. The word freemium implies selling a basic configuration (or a limited time full license) of a product for free or at a low price and then selling an upgraded version (or extra time) for a certain price.

Popular for software and online gaming products, this model's only challenge is to ensure that the client likes (or gets addicted to) the product so much that he/she ultimately buys the extended version to help the company monetize. In other words, freemium does enable the customer to try out an application for free and examine the important functionalities before buying the application and paying for the additional value. Even the fact that a customer's eyeballs stayed on a particular site is considered an important metric and sometimes is regarded as important as any downstream monetization.

Coupons are also great value enablers as they discount the product for prospective customers. A low price helps lower the bar for trying out the product, similar to a freemium offering. Very similar to coupons (but somewhat more loyalty forming) is establishing a members' club and encouraging card use for receiving discounted pricing offers.

Entrepreneurs can also adopt a paradigm completely different from what the existing (and larger) market players use. For example, the SaaS vendors went about understanding the value of the benefits their services brought forth before pricing their services for different functionalities, or tiers of users.

The advent of the Internet has leveled the playing field quite a bit and has significantly reduced the middleman's portion, thus helping the manufacturer in pricing by selling direct from the warehouse.

At the other end, companies such as Reliance in India have been investing in local sourcing to keep the prices low. Along with maintaining the prices low, it also helps in keeping the merchandize fresh, farmers happy and the local economy growing.

BUILDING ON BRAND AND PRODUCT REDESIGN

While education helps customers, and entrepreneurs, realize pains and unmet needs, enabling lets customers know what a pain-relief solution is worth. Enabling also establishes why the entrepreneur's products relieve pain better than the others. And that it does through brand building. Brand is perhaps the single most important way to enable prospective customers to know about a product and establish positive association with that product.

Brand equity describes the importance of having a well-known brand name and how that enables product differentiation (quality, features, personality, and other emotional benefits); how that makes the product popular and customers aware; and ultimately how that helps customers be loyal to the product thereby expanding the market share.

One of the key enabling efforts by the enabling team is to raise the brand awareness, which is also a measure of the extent of recognition of a brand among prospective customers. The other is to raise the brand loyalty so that customers buy products from the entrepreneur over and over, and not from other suppliers. A strong brand eases the sale of the product or service, by removing a lot of decision-making need when the customer is about to make a purchase decision. The customer already knows about the brand and hence the product. Remember our discussion on how a franchisee benefits due to the brand as that reflects a standard product.

Brand building starts during the Educate phase (when a solution is anchored in the customer's brain), but grows on these prospects/customers during the Enable phase as this is when the firm builds on the existing brand image (which can disappear if not attended to) and strengthens the awareness and loyalty. So you may have planted the seed earlier, but now is the time to water and provide nourishment for its growth. Most of the time this is an iterative process—you tell your customer about your product (educate), where to get them or how to use (enable), and then the customer tells you what more your product needs to have (educate). Accordingly, you make a change in the product to help the customer (enable).

This change in the product to fulfill these customer needs, require the entrepreneur to revisit the product design and refine the specifications. Some agile product development processes call for "sprints" to add functionality in an iterative way, as the minimum viable product evolves to reach the MVP.

Brand building involves a big-picture marketing plan that integrates company, and product goals. Brand presents the values, and attributes of a company and helps the customer to position the company and its products in his mind. This means a much greater emphasis on the customer, and adapting all products and services to fit his changing needs and behavior.

As branding is strategic, several years of marketing effort is needed to build a solid brand. Strong brand, however, helps make the marketing easy and less expensive if the prospect is educated already through personal experience, recommendations from friends, testimonials or advertisements. In other words, a strong brand converts people looking for solutions to customers, and makes existing customers evangelists.

Also the stronger the brand is, the more its credibility within its markets. The media you chose to advertise in, and your promotions can also greatly affect how your brand is perceived by potential customers.

While some companies brand their businesses to offer the lowest prices, others brand themselves as having superior quality. Virtual/social vehicles can help the brand-building process enormously, particularly customer reviews and friends talking about the product over a social site. Blogs, too, add to the image of the product quality. Kabob Times, which projected the restaurant as a Middle Eastern experience provider, managed to handle expectations well by attending constantly to these vehicles.

Perhaps it is important to talk about the role of public relations (or PR) also at this point as entrepreneurs are increasingly using PR organizations or in-house public relations departments to spread information to the prospective customer. PR has become almost as valuable a tool as advertising for entrepreneurs with limited budgets as it helps the brand-building process by influencing the media. PR, in some cases, comes for no cost, particularly for groundbreaking products and services.

Figure 3.4 Brand and Design Iteration from Educate to Enable

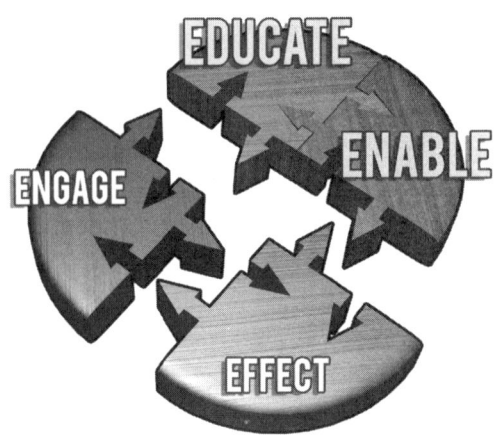

Lately, the PR agencies have become increasingly active on the Internet, particularly in the blogging and social media realm (beyond TV, radio, and magazines).

ADVERTISING REACH AND CAMPAIGNS

Advertising helps increase brand awareness, and build brand loyalty, by bringing the uniqueness of the product in front of the prospective customers. Advertising enables prospects to know of promotions; updates on new features, upgrades, and services; and other differentiable areas. While the message is central to all advertising as that conveys the benefit to the consumer, it has to bring out the product positioning in the most creative way. Finding the right media, identifying the reach to prospects, the frequency of exposure of a message and the impact of the exposure through a given media are some of the significant tasks for the enabling team.

The entrepreneur's focus remains on utilizing his limited budget in the most profitable way and so he has to decide on the message, reach, frequency, impact and geography. A bigger question the entrepreneur faces today is around the optimum media mix, or in other words, how much in resources should be put on new media versus traditional?

TRADITIONAL MEDIA

According to a 2013 report produced at the USC Marshall School of Business, consumption of traditional media (TV, radio, and so on) is estimated to reach a whopping 1.7 trillion hours by 2015. That translates to more than 15 hours per person per day.

Figure 3.5 Advertising

According to the study, hours of consumption rose close to 5 percent a year from 2008–2013 due to more viewing hours from 11 hours per day to an average of over 14 hours per day, and population growth.

Source: http://www.marshall.usc.edu/faculty/centers/ctm/research/how-much-media (Accessed on November 3, 2015).

Traditional media over the years has developed solid, well-crafted content. Along with it, it has also created a widespread audience. It has spent decades in cultivating these interests worldwide across various segments for vastly differing topics. That has made traditional media expert at knowing the customer segments for their programs. Moreover, these customer segments trust the traditional media as even with the advent of the latest social/new-media-friendly devices, customers are still linking to the content developed for traditional media.

There is a lot of information that is being produced due to new media, especially on the Internet. And as a result, people are looking to get information from news sources they trust.

Source: http://www.forbes.com/sites#/sites/jeffbercovici/ 2013/06/06/cbs-anchor-scott-pelley-on-the-surprising- renaissance-of-the-evening-news/ (Accessed on November 3, 2015).

NEW MEDIA

Increasingly, teenagers have reported learning about current events from social media sites as opposed to newspapers.

Social media, as the name suggests, is socially developed media and to a great extent is fed by content from everyone. Now, as this includes everyone (or everyone who has access to a PC or a mobile device), marketers (particularly enablers) are very interested. Broadly speaking, the dominant social media types include:

1. Crowdsourcing (Wikipedia, *The Huffington Post*)
2. Blog/self-updates (Blogger, Twitter)
3. Broadcast (YouTube)
4. Social networking (Facebook, LinkedIn)

In a social media environment, entrepreneurs can promote their product and improve their company's brand by interacting with users and molding their viewpoints about the product. More consumers are accessing social media today via mobile platforms. If you combine social media with smart devices, we see hundreds of ways of spreading facts about new products or services at a very low cost.

Social networking sites such as Facebook, LinkedIn, YouTube, and Twitter provide constant alternative news sources for users. Social media will keep increasing the information disparity between marketers using modern technology and those who do not understand or apply new technologies.

Kabob Times started late on this road. It implemented social media tracking tools to analyze who is saying what about their products and services. It helped Suzanne, the owner, identify new areas that she had never before tapped. Although she was not very happy with the quality of the content on these sites, she loved the reach it gave her without costing an arm and a leg. She, however, was not ecstatic about the fact that social media was like a conversation that everyone participated in but nobody got to control (very similar to the weather, except that in the case of social media conversation gets started by humans). That is why it was difficult to let any marketing message out at first; however, she became successful when she made friends, and gradually introduced her services as she started to enter people's trust circles.

Kabob Times took advantage of the "real-time" nature of social media, as well, particularly as the restaurant communicated with a large number of people in its circle. Then these people further communicated with others in their circles, thus expanding the reach and allowing loyal

Figure 3.6 Traditional Versus New

customers to be evangelists and marketers for its business. The closer Kabob Times got to the customers through these conversations, the more effective they became.

But Kabob Times was not dependent on social media alone. In fact, Suzanne started with print ads in the local newspapers. She felt that it added to the restaurant's credibility, since these papers were read by a demographic that made important household purchase decisions. Although the advertisement posting price was much higher than for social media, the ads and the coupons supplied through the newspaper brought the critical mass of diners to Kabob Times and helped it cross a chasm. Shortly thereafter, Kabob Times started email and social media campaigns. This initial group of loyal customers helped the business grow and brought others into the conversation.

Suzanne also used a re-targeting service, so that even after a prospect left the Kabob Times' website they were reminded of coupons and other promotions. Kabob Times also very frequently updated the YouTube posts with new promotions and video reviews of customers. More social media members became attracted to Kabob Times. They wrote, commented, invited others and thus engaged in growing the group—and that too at no extra cost. Those customers genuinely felt that the quality of food and the ambience (and other aspects) deserved mention and that others should at least give that place a try.

The other thing that evangelists (or the group of very loyal customers) did for Kabob Times was to build the brand with their personal recommendations (without hoping to get anything in return for doing that). That loyalty, in turn, really strengthened the image of Kabob Times as "a provider of high quality food and a very engaging dinner experience".

Suzanne also started writing a weekly article for a local newspaper on interesting experiments in her kitchen—something that she felt her customers would value, and connect with. Most of these were time-saving preparations (dishes you can cook under five minutes) and then she also included gourmet preparations from the readers. She gathered readers and writers this way and spread the word even faster.

Suzanne also started emailing links to the blog and other communications to prospective and existing customers once a month. That was a great way to keep them updated with new recipes, and inform them of events and parties that interested the demographic.

KICKING OFF LOGISTICS

The Enabler gets the customer interested in the product by explaining in detail the value that the product brings to the customer. More importantly, the enabler also makes the product available to the customer on a timely basis and at a reasonable cost. And for that the enabler has to plan the delivery and logistics elaborately and carefully.

Channels have grown over time, and they continue to evolve with new needs and technologies. Distribution systems can have multiple tiers between the entrepreneur and the end user. As every level takes a bite in the entrepreneur's margin, there is a continuous pressure to reduce the number of tiers. However, when distance or access to remote places become difficult, the entrepreneur looks for outside help. For example, customized services by a middleman (or VARs) can increase the pie size. This model is beneficial for the entrepreneur both from sales as well as logistical perspectives as he does not have to be involved in them and the company still grows.

Entrepreneurs typically subscribe to trade magazines and visit tradeshows. Such places get the attention of more prospective buyers and middlemen, and entrepreneurs learn about new practices and preferred ways of distribution in the industry. The primary challenge for an entrepreneur who wants to tap a new geography, or introduce a new service is to adapt the service to cater to that region/district. The entrepreneur also customizes the packaging, pricing, giving away of samples and conducting new promotions for different markets. For example, McDonald's in India has a somewhat different product line as it caters to a non-beef eating population there.

McDonalds' has menu items for local tastes, such as the Maharaja Mac with chicken as the meat and McAloo Tikki with a spicy potato patties. McDonalds' also plans to open vegetarian-only restaurants to cater to the 40 percent of Indian population that does not eat meat.

Source: http://www.cbsnews.com/news/mcdonalds-to-beef-up-in-india-with-meatless-menu/ (Accessed on November 3, 2015).

As entrepreneurs use a variety of ways to promote the product (new media as well as traditional media), the message has to include ease of product purchase, delivery and implementation. With the advent of Internet commerce, it has become easier for the entrepreneurs to open a virtual store and use third party services for payment and shipping. Even sourcing is easier due to the Internet, and so is connecting directly with global service providers.

In its effort to enable, Kabob Times had launched a separate food truck business and had developed a website for it. The website published the menu, and the schedule (dates and times) of their truck locations. Apart from that, Kabob Times also started an online food business where they took orders from a website and fulfilled them from a warehouse.

Between multiple lines of business, the traffic the website generated was remarkable and so was the crowd that the truck business drew. Suzanne was convinced, at that point, that she had built some brand loyalty to take the company to the next level—franchising and partnerships.

After Kabob Times entered into partnerships and franchises, some of the logistics got taken care of by the partners and franchisees. However, the Kabob Times

Figure 3.7 Kabob Times Enabling Multiple Customer Bases

franchising team, which was being headed by Cyrus (the chef), constantly coached and mentored these partners and franchisees and shared updated menus. Kabob Times was still responsible for sending across the Tahini and Tzatziki sauce mixes to the franchisees, and ensure the franchisees followed the operating procedures and cooking standards laid out by Kabob Times.

For Figaro, sales agents did a major portion of the selling through mail order catalogs, and then through distributors and other sales channels. They were also supported by the customer service department. They started with media exposure (using a PR firm) to jumpstart the sales.

Figaro also started a website, a Facebook site, and several satellite sites for its range of products. It hired a search engine optimization consultant and kept an online sales team for email and web marketing to get its product out to more people.

***

You may have noticed how tightly sales and distribution (or sales and delivery) are intertwined and at times it is difficult to draw a line between them. Take the case of franchising and then certain forms of partnerships—where the sales and distribution are done by some other company as part of a pre-agreed contract or just for commission.

This is the reason almost everyone in the Four E framework can market and sell. The central idea is to see how we are engaging the customer for the longer haul through the framework. An educator sells at tradeshows and other educational events. An effecter is a hunter searching for suspects, and prospects and closing the sale; and an engager is the farmer, who maintains relationships with existing customers and cross-sells and up-sells other services and products missing to the customers. An enabler sells by making sure product is scoped right, priced aptly, distributed so that it is accessible even at remote locations, and promoted fittingly.

While we have already looked at product design, promotion and pricing for enabling the customers, let us look at some of the retail market middle-layers, who play a role in sales and in getting the products distributed to the retailers or directly to consumers.

Independent representatives: Independent salespeople work commonly on commission, represent many companies, and work closely with the seller.

Brokers: A broker works on commission and has a range of competing products so that buyers can have several options.

Private label/licensing: Entrepreneurs sell to leading brands or license from them in order to be marketed as a part of their line.

Wholesalers: Wholesalers, traditionally, were the stage before a product went to the retail stores.

Figure 3.8 The Middlemen

Remember, every layer takes a cut, so you have to man-ufacture the product at a very low cost to make it priced right for the end customer and to get it enough space on the shelves of a retail store. With Internet and new media, however, access between end customers and manufactur-ers has become direct. If you look at the models for Etsy and eBay, they provide a marketplace to sellers and buy-ers without the need for layers of middlemen or whole-salers. Although the touch and feel factor is missing from Internet marketplaces, it certainly helps in keeping mar-gins high for the sellers and prices low for the customers.

ENABLE CHARACTERISTICS

For an entrepreneurial firm, the enablers are the level-headed individuals who understand the big picture, and work on long-term returns. They take marketing strategy roles. They understand the vision of the entrepreneur and the need of the customer and act as enablers of the com-pany's ideas, and need-fulfillment to get the product out to prospective customers in the most optimum and satisfac-tion-rendering way.

The enablers also influence prospect customers effec-tively by understanding them, creating value for them, building brand awareness, conducting high ROI advertis-ing and efficiently working logistics.

So what skills are important for an enabler? A highly skilled enabling team should possess the following skill sets:

1. Survey and data interpretation: An essential skill needed for enabling is the ability to conduct surveys, run analytics and interpret the responses to get to meaningful outcomes. With big data crunching and

predictive analytics becoming so necessary, this
skill is very important.

2. Empathizing: Understanding changing priorities of
prospects is important for enablers in order to get
closer to customers and fulfill their NEW needs.

3. Pricing expertise: Identifying the value and price
that customers are willing to pay for the product
is significant—particularly for setting reasonable
prices.

4. Brand equity building knowhow: Being able to
develop a brand and generate brand awareness
helps customers in associating positive attributes
with the product. A strong brand also means low
spending on logistics and promotions. This is a great
skill to have.

5. Advertising, PR and promotion expertise: No matter
how strong the brand is, the enabler has to spend
some time and effort in advertising and promoting
products/services. Advertising also helps increase
the brand awareness. PR skills help spread great-
ness in a more cost effective way.

6. Logistics abilities: Another skill is the ability to
coordinate logistics and work with the right tiers
and partners to ensure the users get the best experience and the business still derives the maximum
margin.

CHAPTER SUMMARY

The Educate Phase brought us closer to the needs of the
customers. It also helped us in reaching out to prospect
customers and informing them about the new products
as well as those in the pipeline. The interaction helped us

understand the engaging zone between the entrepreneur and the customer.

The Enable phase takes the understanding of customer's product needs even further. You start building the engaging zone that works for you, the entrepreneur, as well as for the customer.

Enable phase looks at qualifying leads, and identifying who can be considered a potential customer. Based on that, the Enabler identifies ways to categorize the prospective customer. In order to do that, the enabler identifies the value system that defines the prospective customer, and what pleases him. That gives the enabler an understanding of the different categories of customers he is dealing with. Armed with that, he buckets these prospective customers into segments so that he can enable them in each segment in the most optimum way.

The enabler works closely with the educator on the product price. If the product calls for value-based pricing, the enabler looks at the customer's willingness to pay for the solution to their pain. Another way to look at it is to factor in the reference price (the price of the old/ existing solution), revenue increase (increase in revenues for the customers from the use of the new product) and cost savings (reduction in customer costs from the use of new product). If it is market pricing, the enabler can use other methods to be in the same ballpark as competing products. Enablers can adopt freemium ways to get the prospective customer to try before they buy or discounts to lower the bar for them to try the product.

Closely linked to pricing is brand and product redesign. Brand enables product differentiation, and builds positive association for customers thereby building customer's trust in the product. This is an iterative process— you tell your customer about your product (educate) and where to get them or how to use them (enable) and then the customer tells you what more your product needs to have (educate). Accordingly you make a change in the product to help the customer (enable).

Brand building takes several years of marketing effort. Strong brand, however, helps make marketing easy, and less expensive, as the prospect is educated and enabled. The media you choose to advertise in and the promotions, also greatly affects how your brand is perceived by potential customers.

While the message is central to all advertising as that conveys the benefit to the consumer, it has also to bring out the product positioning in the most creative way. Finding the right media, identifying the reach to prospects, the frequency of exposure of a message and the impact of the exposure through a given media are some of the most important tasks for the enabling team.

Traditional media over the years has developed solid, well-crafted content. Along with it, it has also created a widespread audience. New Media—and particularly social networking sites—will keep increasing the information disparity between marketers using modern technology and those who do not understand or apply new technologies.

The Enable phase besides getting the customer informed about, and interested in the product also makes it available on a timely basis and at a reasonable cost. But the entrepreneur has to plan the delivery and logistics elaborately and carefully. Channels have grown over time, and they continue to evolve with new needs and technologies. Distribution systems can have multiple tiers between the entrepreneur and the end user. There is a continuous pressure to reduce the number of tiers for the entrepreneur, but when distance or access to remote places become difficult, the entrepreneur looks for out-side help—partners, VAR resellers, and franchisees.

The next chapter on the Effect phase adds to all you have learned while reading the chapters on *Educate* and *Enable*, and adds an extra dimension to that.

Effect is about closing a sale, completing the product design, effecting a change in a status quo, bringing the results to fruition, and getting the customers into the engaging zone.

Effecting is about ensuring that the burn rate is within limits and customers are still interested and vetting the product modifications. Effecting is also about hustling to produce an outcome that is good for the entrepreneur and for customers.

Figure 3.9 Your DogFood, LLC

Case Study—Your DogFood, LLC.

Let us consider you have created a dog food after arduous research requiring labor and careful and endless observation of what led your pet, Tommy, to be a superdog. You found that it was all in the food (in other words, no matter how much your dog attends to muscle toning and agility building through traditional ball-fetching routines, food is what determined ultimate health). As has been the theme of innovator-entrepreneur stories, you want your formula to succeed and you do not have a lot of funds. Let us add the fact that you have been able to do some education already in a pilot market (your zip code or even your town). Now, the question is: how would you start enabling your business and other dog owners, and never have to see dogs being malnourished.

During the last four months, you have been attending all events in the neighborhood and visiting farmers' markets every week. You then develop copy, and images that clearly explain how the amino acids in your flagship product target the key muscle groups of dogs. You also elaborate that protein absorption is the key and though there are other products in the market, yours is the only one which has proteins that get easily absorbed. That is your product's competitive advantage. You also create an animated display as a collateral item which shows a liquid flowing into the body and most of it clings to the muscles. The display and your conversations with people create a group of interested parties. We call them leads.

(Continued)

(Continued)

Your closest friend, Brenda, is the enabler. She picks up that list of leads and looks at other information elicited from the questionnaire you asked them to complete in exchange for getting their names for a lucky draw (and your leads' list). Brenda identifies the truly interested parties (calls them prospects) from the list and groups them under two categories—big dogs and small dogs, as you have different products for these two groups. Brenda also looks at other data in the questionnaire and builds a list of what the customers miss in the current offerings and would like to have in a product.

The questionnaire also provides you information on their willingness to pay. You had given out free trial packets and other promotions when you were collecting information. So, now is the time to call them back and ask a few more questions (in the bidirectional spirit of the Four E framework). What questions would you ask?

You have visited all the local pet-food shops and you have an idea of the prices of competing products. If you have some unique delivery methodology or some exclusive patented ingredient then you can solely look at the willingness to pay numbers from the questionnaire. But, most likely, you have to see what others are charging for similar products and what is the cost to produce yours. Using a combination of these inputs, you go ahead and start pricing and you run those by a group in your pilot market. Based on the feedback, you build a price list that has prices set for different points of sale, geographies, agents selling the product, delivery methods, ordering interfaces, among others. Who do you want to share this price list with?

While Brenda was building the price list, you have been approaching another group of customers in your pilot market (bidirectional spirit is all about sharing some and gathering some) and asking them about the product and also checking their brand loyalty. You change the packaging and the taste as per the feedback you receive and also ask them how comfortable they are to buy these products for their friends. How do you make them respond to that question affirmatively?

Brenda starts asking the group about the promotions that they look forward to (coupons, getting a free packet with every packet they buy, among other options). And how do they get information on these promotions (the fliers they receive in the mail, heard it on radio, notices on supermarket bulletin boards, word of mouth, among others).

Based on this situation, you plan your campaign starting with an email blast where you include coupons that can be downloaded. You advertise in the local newspaper and submit press releases. You also establish your presence on social media sites and you incentivize prospects for sharing or declaring that they "like" the product. How do you deal with prospects who write negative comments about your product?

(Continued)

(Continued)

You had already started talking to independent sales representatives, brokers, retailers, and wholesalers in an effort to see if they can carry your product and sell it for a cut. They may suggest changes as well (around packaging and delivering), and then you have to make those changes. They may come back and tell you that none of the retailers are ready to stock your product. What would you do?

You also build a partnership network, and work with some of the other product makers in the same industry to hedge your options. You also look at possible options to co-market or co-promote. Franchising may be an option for you as well if you decide to start a retail shop, sell those products and some add-on services (dog shampooing and so on); or you can go to a product maker and license your idea in exchange for a royalty on sales. What would you do if none of these sales/distribution relationships work out?

Some of these answers will be better answered in the next chapters but the enable aspect will enable generating a product that is produced and priced right (both for you and for the customer). The enable phase also aims at exposing the product aptly to the customer (through advertising, public relations, promotions, and brand building), and ensuring that the customers get access to it (through sales and distribution channels). Although some of the sales/distribution channels handle some of the sales, particularly for products that customers are well-educated about; the next phase (effect phase) handles the more complex sales closing for products and services.

4

Effect(uate) Phase

As per Webster, Effect (verb \i-ˈfekt, e-, ē-, ə-\) or effectuate implies to cause (something), to make (something) happen, to cause (something) to produce the desired result.

Most dictionaries use effect and effectuate interchangeably. For the most part, we will treat them as interchangeable as well, except for some aspects where the effectual aspect has a special meaning for entrepreneurs, as we draw on some studies conducted on that front.

Going back to the war of Kurukshetra, it took 18 days to end the war; however, every move was tactical. In other words, the plans evolved incrementally. The central goal of winning the war, however, was unchanged. And Krishna was the effecter who brought about all the moves and made the victory possible. Effecting (effectuating) is a lot about making things happen tactically, and iteratively to get to the strategic goal.

Effecting something (such as closing a sale or development of a product) depends a lot on attitude/passion, culture, big picture or strategic understanding and available resources as well as the environment. Effecting also implies being disruptive and adopting a hustler mentality to build something—perhaps of limited value initially but adding more value incrementally and iteratively.

Needless to say, beyond the effecter, the environment also contributes to making a want a need, and hence plays a big role in effectuation. Innovations get incorporated into the social fiber, and people participate in those changes. As a result, we see products built to solve only one problem evolve to address multiple problems.

An effecter's contribution can also be considered similar to a finance chief, who carefully oversees the developments and elongates the crests and reduce the troughs in the uncertainties of engagement. The adapting is done by changing parameters of the product such as price, advertising, promotion, geographies, distribution process, sales, or the product itself. A cycle of enable-effect-enable (bidirectional theme) helps the effecter get to a stabler outcome of what the customer would like in a final product (or to effect a sale). That essentially has a lower risk than building a complex product without vetting the same with the client and realizing the absence of true customers or need of major changes at the very end when there is no money left.

"It is not the strong, nor the intelligent who survive," wrote Charles Darwin, "but those who are quickest to adapt." The typical Effect activities are driven by the effecter's quick to adapt attitude and big-picture vision.

The central theme again is to get the customers into the engaging zone or the zone, which the educators identified as a negotiating point. This is where both customer and entrepreneur see value in a transaction. The enabler took the specification and worked on the parameters and developed the engaging zone. The effecter works closely with the customer to tweak the product parameters and finally get the customer to agree and buy. For price-sensitive customers, he identifies how to lower the price even if that means giving away some functionality.

For functionality-craving customers, he does away with resources spent on the look and feel.

Ideas can come from various sources of inspiration. Perhaps a friend told you about an interesting idea. You pursued this idea to create a specific product and then got a patent. In another scenario, an older friend or family member told you about an old process of paint patch up for cars. Intrigued, you spoke with a manufacturer and they were ready to produce an updated version. Your neighbor did something extraordinary to water his lawn and you wondered how it could be done better. You built upon that concept, patented it, and licensed the product idea.

No matter how the idea comes to you, the important thing is to develop it and then take it to market. Make it useful for the customer (serving an important utility) and commercially viable, so that customers can get exposed to the product and buy it. In other words, if you create and put something new in the market, people may actually try the item out. But to get it to a retail/online shop, and have prospective customers try or buy it requires a good amount of effecting (along with educating, and enabling) to stay on target without burning too much.

In the case of coupons, they were created by innovators to help consumers try products and perhaps become loyal. The latter part is not true of course—the couponing generation of today could never be loyal to a product/service (they are only loyal to couponing). So, now how do we get our customers addicted and make them loyal to our product?

Let us talk about the roles of the phases once again with some more attributes. The Educate phase is where a firm innovates as per the need of the market (identifying the engaging zone) and at the same time disseminates information about existing products. Enable is to further understand the customers (and build that engaging zone using

Figure 4.1 Effect

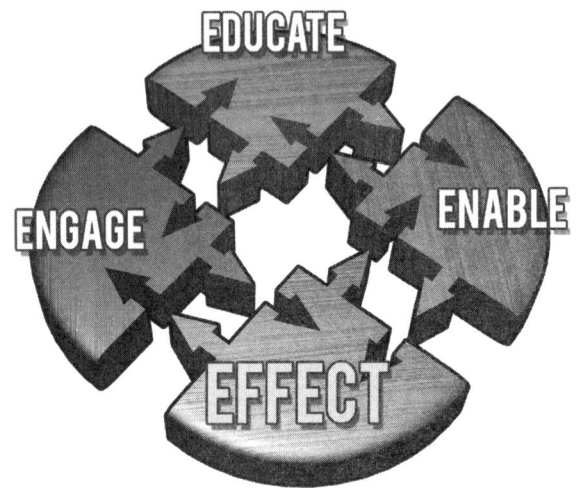

product parameters) and reach them in the best possible way. There is a small iterative process in educate-enable-educate as some of the learning that gets done about the customer goes into product refinement and toward enabling the customer.

The Effect phase takes the outreach process to the next level and brings the need fulfillment into action. It, thus, brings customers into the engaging zone. Another iteration happens here to ensure customers bless the product or buy the idea through an enable-effect-enable cycle or even educate-enable-effect-educate cycle.

Dealing with existing customers (or prospects who have said yes to the product idea) and upselling them new ideas is easier than acquiring new customers (by educating, enabling and effecting). Therefore, the phase that follows the Effect phase is the Engage phase where our goal is to keep customers in the engaging zone. Effect in our framework is about ensuring the customer understands the solution and has bought into it. The final goal again is to engage so as to have a steady stream of revenue from the engaged and hence loyal customers.

If the education and enabling are done right, the Effect phase becomes much easier. The effecter's role is more sales oriented in the service business (compared to most consumer product businesses) as almost all service and business-to-business product contracts require a negotiated understanding between two parties before the sale is actually made. For consumer products, the effecter's role is to get inside the minds of the prospect customer and then establish a value for the solution.

Effecters are therefore called upon for deal closure, or for finalizing the product/solution, as their expertise lies in ensuring that the prospective customer is convinced that the sale is a bargain, or the product will address their pain points. Thus, effecting is placed as a spontaneous performance to get the prospects into the engaging zone.

Figure 4.2 Effecter and Engaging Zone

As prospects get educated, and enabled, the effecter leverages that learning to further talk about product areas that interest the prospect customer. Educating and enabling help the scoping of the product (or solution) as they determine what some of the pain points are, and identify what likely remediation methods are. With no assurance that educated and enabled prospects will get engaged for the long term, effecters improvise (or pivot) and experiment with new ideas, remain flexible to the end goal, and then capture the successes in a model and replicate it.

When Pandora was launched in 2000, with an idea to license the service to major search engines, they took calculated risks. In time the model changed as the company experimented by changing the different levers and it found that servicing the consumers directly had better outcomes. Subsequent to that, the business changed its delivery model and today is one of the leading music streaming services.

Successful entrepreneurs are more likely to effectuate, so they experiment with an idea, build a product, and then pivot as required. Pandora was launched in early 2000 with a B-to-B business model, switched over to a B-C model, and then to a third model.

Source: http://entreprof.com/effectual-logic-entrepreneurs/ (Accessed on November 3, 2015).

Effecters create a successful business even when faced by a host of uncertainties: unknown market size, unidentified customer segments, unfamiliar competition and new technologies, among other factors. As the effecters are solid risk managers they are stringent about their means and can reduce the burn rate, get customer buy in and build a product liked by the customer.

By gauging customer reaction at each step, and making incremental improvements, the right value can be incorporated. As a result, these effecters take a very agile approach to starting with an idea. They create the minimum viable product and then iteratively get it to the MVP to best respond to customer needs.

Extensive research around effectual entrepreneurship, conducted by Dr Saras Sarasvathy, professor in strategy, entrepreneurship and ethics at the University of Virginia's Darden School of Business along with other thought leaders, has identified a number of principles that guide effectual entrepreneurs, mainly around:

- Starting without waiting for everything to be in order, and for specs to be defined.
- Setting stop-loss points, and basing the evaluation decisions on acceptable downside as opposed to the upside.
- Remaining flexible regarding goals, and being prepared to embrace surprises.
- Working with elements within control, and creating opportunities.

Due to the effectual thought process, entrepreneurs believe in a yet-to-be-made future that still needs to be shaped by execution and they realize that this human execution could control the future. So much so that it is better to work closely with those engaged in decisions rather than working to predict the future.

(Continued)

(*Continued*)

> *Source:* http://www.effectuation.org/sites/default/files/
> documents/what-makes-entrepreneurs-entrepreneurial-
> sarasvathy.pdf (Accessed on November 3, 2015).

Kabob Times started without specific goals (do not get me wrong—the company did want to be profitable). Suzanne loved socializing particularly in her Middle Eastern circle and partnered with Cyrus, a chef who specialized in Lebanese food. But after talking to the customers, they saw that focusing on Middle Eastern food with a hookah lounge would make the greatest impact. They did just that and it was success at a low burn rate.

The other remarkable thing about Suzanne's restaurant enterprise was how it kept itself agile and forward looking without focusing too much on one service. Suzanne looked at all possible locations where she could spread the word: ethnic (Middle Eastern and Asian) groceries, belly dancing studios, and similar places. She worked a commission deal with some of these retail shops and at others she posted pamphlets with coupons and discounts.

Then the business started food delivery. Initially, Suzanne did not charge a delivery fee for food, and she used to send one of her employees to deliver the orders. However, as she gathered a strong foothold in the market and established brand awareness in the area, she used a third party delivery company to deliver food. She had to open a separate takeout shop focused on deliveries and takeout.

Suzanne took calculated risks—another effecter quality. Like every other business she had to embrace uncertainties such as having no assurance if she would get enough customers to meet the burn rate. Then there were other smaller improbabilities such as having no idea as to how helpful the neighboring Chinese restaurant was or even if there was enough parking for all the retail shops in the strip mall. But, she knew for sure that if the customers were engaged they would come back for more, and so she kept herself open to incremental evolution.

Suzanne did not start with an assumption that she would get 100 customers every day and that every customer would buy food worth $100 dollars. She considered the worst case and used a burn rate to calculate how many months she would be able to operate the business before she ran out of money.

The other effecter trait that Suzanne showed was her openness to experiment. When she heard from a friend of hers that he needed a place to host social events, she immediately acted on the idea, and started conducting social events in the restaurant in the afternoons and non-peak hours. She also used the vast space she had for dance lessons during non-peak hours. And that effected more engagement.

A conversation with Stuart Read, at IMD, about how expert entrepreneurs work effectually to achieve success came forth with some interesting points, including: (a) they work with what they have to get going, (b) they focus on partnerships rather than competition during the early stages; (c) they look at the worst case while taking risks; and (d) they see an opportunity even when a surprise hits their plans.

Source: http://www.livemint.com/Companies/ MtdMBfWPWwO12p3iPelf8M/Stuart-Read--Expert- entrepreneurs-make-it-okay-for-themselv.html (Accessed on November 3, 2015).

SALES FORECASTING, TEAMING, AND COACHING

The effecters are the rainmakers. They understand the customer and then the customer's customer. They are part of almost all marketing promotions and campaigns and are thoroughly conversant with customer behavior. However, beyond getting the prospective customers into the engaging zone (or closing a sale), they also attend to some other details which we will cover in this section.

FORECASTING SALES

For a small business, sales forecasting can be as simple as tracking the number of products sold at different times of a day. For a larger business, however, it could mean building a model for trending sales against the existing players. With several dynamically changing parameters, it is even more difficult to get sales' forecasts perfect. But a lot can be done to get them into a reasonable ballpark.

Factors affecting sales include economic cycles, changing customer behavior, competition from unforeseen quarters, and increases in the cost of goods. Bad sales' forecasts can cause too much or too little inventory, both of which land the business into a difficult situation. Likewise, neither seeing the emerging competition nor future costs can force a firm to take the wrong direction. So the effecters have to be cognizant of all these factors while coming up with the forecast.

Effecters start the process by forecasting unit sales per month using past data. If they have no data (e.g., if this is a new product), the effecters use a similar product's historical data. If the line of business does not lend itself to unit sales per month (e.g., an engineering services' firm that take on projects of varying sizes that are difficult to trend), the effecters need to sit with enablers, and engagers, to analyze the firm's opportunity data by looking at the sales funnel and opportunities from evolving relationships and outstanding proposals.

A forecast can be used as a tool to tweak the goals and at the same time manage resources. It is something that has to be revisited almost every week to see how the big-picture plan is working out. Add to that the fact that forecasting should always be a collaborative process, and the educators, enablers, engagers, and effecters should all be contributing to it.

The modern-day CRM allows collaboration of the different groups, and tracks services, products, geographies, accounts, opportunities, and sales representatives. It also helps in identifying exceptions where the forecast does not fall in the same ballpark as the actual sales data, and in finding areas for improvement.

COOPETITION

Teaming benefits all entrepreneurs. An effecter understands the need of partnering within and outside the teams, particularly if the scale of sale is impossible for the entrepreneur to accomplish alone. When GXXview planned to come up with a viewing subscription product and scoped entire Southern California, it took help from leading firms and universities in the area. The GXXview executives led the product development by ensuring they had buy-in from key influencers in the industry. This teaming decision not only helped the company in brand building, it also catapulted the effecter's efforts in responding to the opportunity.

The ecosystem allows for such entrepreneurs to work with other entrepreneurs, and with larger corporations to broaden their service offerings. It can also address any shortage of skills for the entrepreneur as the experience of the partners can always fill the gap. Beyond assisting with skill shortage, partnering also helps entrepreneurs if they are short-staffed. GXXView, for instance, partnered with other firms on government bids and offered its existing customers a longer menu of items to choose from.

Even larger corporations have started to think like entrepreneurs. Often they encourage their business units to work with entrepreneurial firms to get used to some of the practices there. With their employees working with agile startups, the perspectives of large corporations have increasingly changed toward problem-solving. This has helped them come up with simpler solutions by avoiding some of the unnecessary bureaucracy that corporations get used to. It also accomplishes going faster to the root of the problem and resolving it in the most cost-effective way.

So, the next time you attend a conference and chance upon another entrepreneur in the same business, chances are that you will combine forces and not compete with each other.

WTF JUST HAPPENED PHENOMENON AND COACHING

As we discussed earlier, "WTF just happened" moment is a phenomenon most commonly noticed in firms that do not have robust plan Bs to manage an unexpected outcome.

Let us consider an example. Almost a month before Black Friday, you had 50 new customers sign up on your website for a product that you had launched for Black Friday (you had just started and so you had not expected clients would register to that extent). You were pleasantly surprised at your sharpness or perhaps a point that clients saw value in. That is when you started thinking why cannot other folks sell as well as you do and you started forcing yourself to evaluate how you differentiated yourself from them, and also what should these other guys do to keep up with your prowess. And then at the All Hands meeting you were a hero. New joiners started taking notes when you spoke, particularly when you talked about how you did a quick analysis and estimated the lifetime value for these clients.

But then Friday came, and most of the clients who had signed up cancelled their service. You had no idea what happened. That is known as a WTF just happened moment. An effecter in such a case normally wades through the situation, identifies what caused a variance from expected outcome, updates everyone, takes action to correct any wrong perception, and solves the problem.

The effecter understands the need for having plan Bs in the team and building redundancy within the effecter team. So, no matter how important being the rainmaker in the entrepreneurial firm is, it is equally important to transfer these ideas, relationships and strategies to new effecters. By prioritizing the goals of the group, the effecter creates an environment where teamwork thrives and delineation and delegation of tasks are not only clearly understood, but also seriously acted upon.

The senior effecter, thus, always has a solid training plan. In addition to training and experience sharing, key learning comes from participating in real deal closures. In coaching calls, the effecter provides detailed notes on how the discussions went and areas that need further work. The new effecter also gets to explore opportunities to identify customer pain points to aid the senior effecters.

Figure 4.3 Multi-faceted Effecter

A CRM tool helps the effecter with some of these processes, and brings about cadence in the effecter role. It helps in the daily tasks, and can be used to track performance and help the new effecter identify areas that need improvement. Training, however, is most effectively delivered in real time as the new effecters learn different styles and approaches by participating in real work.

FROM OPPORTUNITY HUNTING TO MAKING IT HAPPEN

An effecter is on the constant lookout for product (and sales) opportunities and prospects.

Not all innovation opportunities are, however, feasible. Producing and distributing may not always be cost effective enough. Even the fact that other products exist in the market and which can serve somewhat the same purpose can also deter these effecters. Effecters have limited time and at the earliest stumbling block they face, they have to make a go/no-go decision. As there is a cost of investing time in an opportunity, picking the right one is a key skill that the effecter learns over time.

Limited time and budget necessitate effecters to be great planners—particularly in ranking high return opportunities in the prospecting process. Effecters look into the key traits of prospective customer groups, and see what would make them buy their product/service. Even for product development, effecters gauge how the important stakeholders feel about the final product version. Effecters get help from Enablers to identify solution attributes most attractive to prospective customers (and stakeholders in case of product development). These attributes identify the customers' purchasing power, the demographic/psychographic segments they belong to and their needs or even things such as how often these customers visit different types of websites. Attribute qualifiers or ranges help the effecters decide the types of prospective customers they should focus on.

Identifying "what floats the boat" is not a one-time event. Over time and with changing customer preferences, these attributes change. A CRM tool used by the enabling team drives this aspect for the effecters. They can track the returns, including who the sales team is attending to the most without necessarily getting any wins and who the team is not listening to and possibly missing out on. For example, you have been running scrum meetings for a product that you are sure will cater to health insurance clients. For the sprint review meetings you invite a few of your prospective customers. They show a lot of enthusiasm initially. However, with time their interest in the product fades out and ultimately they do not buy your product. An effecter reduces such incidents.

The effecters start looking closely, using attributes and filters. They put prospective customers in the perceived likelihood buckets (high or low) of getting into the engaging zone. They gather the educator's tradeshow data, the enabler's predictive analytics, and the engager's trend data. Based on all these inputs and analyses, the effecters pick opportunities with the most potential. The effecter queues the opportunities for the effect team members on the basis of geographies, difficulty levels, or familiarity with the client.

The quest then for the effecter is to search for the right individual at the customer's office who values the effecter's services, and influences the buying decision. This influencing individual can be the engineer who looks at a construction project plan and gives his approval, the housewife who wants a food processor, an eight-year-old who likes wheat cereal and bananas, or a parts' buyer for a scanning machine company. These influencers are not the decision makers but play a role in making the final purchase or deciding what the solution should be.

Along with identifying key influencers, and decision makers, the effecter mirrors the thought process of the prospective customers. In other words, the effecter evaluates how much the missing gap means to the prospective customers and how much they are losing in terms of money, image and time in the status quo environment. Even the prospects themselves may not be completely aware of the severity of the problem.

He regularly attends tradeshows and industry meetings, interacts with innovators and prospects, follows social media, looks at new policies and regulations, hobnobs with industry leaders, meets with leading investors and venture capitalists, interacts with his own team of thinkers and visionaries and identifies opportunities. These touch points help the effecter reaffirm the assumptions and identify the value gap even better.

STORYTELLING

The effecters are great at storytelling. They talk about their past, and empathize with the prospects. At times, the effecters share their own mistakes, which in turn builds even more credibility and help prospective customers open up to the effecter. Such relationship establishment takes away any negative bias that the prospect can possibly develop, and helps the effecter in bonding with them.

When Cyrus recommended starting a hookah lounge inside Kabob Times because a corner was not being utilized, Suzanne was thrilled since that would serve as a social meet-up place for over 100 attendees every evening. The hookah lounge did more than just provide a meet-up place. It effected the sharing of people's past experiences (who does not want to tell stuff about themselves if they have an engaged audience?). Suzanne also used to get a platform to speak out her thoughts, which mostly centered on her own flaws. Making fun of her past brought the listeners (and future customers) even closer to Suzanne. A community was created from the hookah lounge, and shortly thereafter came the idea of hosting dance classes there.

Prospects trust research and data. Effecters have command over the subject matter, solid educational backgrounds, and uniquely extensive experience, which make them very credible. They regularly speak in conferences, author white papers in leading journals, and their customers vouch for them.

USING DATA FOR BENCHMARKING AND TRUST-BUILDING

Jeff Kahn, a retail businessman, owned a spa among other retail outfits. In the summer of 2013, he gave a talk at a local community college on how to be successful by spending less than 3 percent of one's salary on grooming oneself. By "grooming", he meant spending toward oneself (e.g., enrolling at a gym, going to a spa every now and then, buying dresses in fashion and dry cleaning them as opposed to washing them at home, among other small expenditures). These efforts can go a long way in establishing a brand image. He shared past experiences that impressed customers, and furthered his personal relationships. For an investment of less than 3 percent of the total salary, a person can achieve these things and get returns that could last a lifetime. Then he gave a few examples of people who were let go because they were always out of style and deemed not to be the leadership type or needed help in organizing their work. Jeff attacked the stem in the brain of his listener—the part that deals with survival.

Jeff also built a definitive pie by putting a number to the spending (3 percent). Jeff shared success stories and gave examples of how often people spend on useless activities and end up spending just as much. With each story and example, the need kept getting anchored in the minds of the audience as they were getting more educated and effected incrementally.

***

When GXXview, the utility GIS firm, started offering an application that showed all engineering data and infrastructure that the municipalities owned on a map (through a cloud application), the company established something unique. It created the first solution of that kind served via the Internet. In addition, the customers did not have to hire resources or buy hardware to install any application.

GXXview improved its offering further and developed a model where it hosted the application for a monthly subscription fee. For a cost of only $2,000 per month, the web application did away with the need to hire a technician and the need to provide that person any training. It was a product that no other firm offered. Hence, there was a big differentiation.

Beyond the low monthly cost (and almost no startup cost), the web application was also accessible from anywhere anytime. In fact, on a rainy night, when a city's power agency faced a major outage, the software helped agency workers locate a key infrastructure document while out in the field. This story was told at paper presentations in multiple conferences by the city's chief engineer. As it was relatable, that effected an immediate trust building among the listeners.

GXXView recounted how their other customers derived returns from implementing some of these solutions in unique ways for various use cases—ways that were not envisioned by GXXview. Cases not ideated while developing the product also came into focus. These new use cases and user-generated stories of how customizable the product was to the needs of the customers also attracted agencies that were looking at solving similar problems. In addition, the presentation also included points around how their application led agencies to being compliant, and following industry best practices. Spelling these points out to show uniqueness helped the effecting team of GXXView position itself well in the minds of prospective customers.

Another way that GXXView made its product more desirable was by establishing scarcity. When it released the product, it announced that it kept the price of the introductory offer at $2,000 per month for the first 50 customers. In the print ad GXXView also mentioned that after the first 50 licenses of the application were sold, the price would go back to its original price of $5,000. This forced scarcity brought about an element of urgency in the prospective customers and they queued up for a piece of this scarce pie.

MAPPING OF BUYING DECISION AND CLOSING

With trust established, the prospective customers get more open about their pains. Fear of system outage failures, lack of management support, and financial concerns were some of the areas where the customers needed more comforting by effecters at GXXView.

The effecter is always ready to help prospective customers who are in need of guidance. Let us go back to the three parts of the brain we discussed earlier: the neocortex, which works with complex thoughts; the limbic system that controls emotions; and then the stem that focuses on the more fundamental function of survival.

The effecter's pitches most often target the stem or the survival instinct. He saves clients from possible overspending, likely failures or even image-related issues. He works closely with prospects, and helps them sell to their supervisors. The effecter does not wait for an opportunity but creates it at the earliest moment he can. He connects his pitch with success stories and also looks at possible price adjustments to help the prospect get into the engaging zone.

We saw how GXXview started pitching the new cloud application, and how the company offered subscriptions to prospect customers at a low price. Similarly, the effecters at ABC Engineering followed a practice to phase out the purchase into multiple years, or with a payment plan best suited to the client. They also offered to run a pilot project to help prospects understand the true value of the solution, and see for themselves the enhanced efficiency in processes. In addition to that, the ABC engineering team shared their past experiences, particularly around staff behavior, with other customers. The ABC team also looked for funding and grants and helped the prospect client with bid documents. Thus making the prospects feel that they were being looked after and not rushed into buying something they did not need.

The effecters did not close the deal then and there. The prospective customer was encouraged to take a deeper look into the proposition and truly understand its value. The effecters also arranged site visits for prospective clients, thus preventing sales stalling or evaporation, while prospects were still making up their minds. In most cases, the prospects came back ready to sign a contract with ABC within a period of three to six months.

EFFECTER CHARACTERISTICS

The effecter team is filled with team members who are personable and are skilled at influencing the influencers. The proverbially aggressive used-car salesperson has gradually faded out. The effecters, now, are exceptional presenters and at the same time great listeners. They are quick to gauge the audience's reaction and change the course of the presentation to something that the audience values and has questions about. The effecters evaluate and act on acceptable downside as opposed to the upside, remain flexible on goals, and are prepared to embrace surprises. The effecter is also passionate about his ideas, is personable and able to make friends easily.

Effecters, who may also be entrepreneurs, make things happen (deal closures, product sale and keeping burn rate low) and have a 360 degree view of how the business operates and what levers are important for growing the business.

Effecters do not wait to be picked, but they pick opportunities on their own. They are the hustlers who charm prospects with their problem-solving attitude, and build trust with their in-depth knowledge.

So what skills are important for an effecter?

1. Agility—Being agile and flexible is very important for an effecter. As the effecter knows a few specifics associated with the outcome of his effort, he has to be agile in his approach and also be prepared for all possible outcomes.

2. Trusted advisor—As the effecter has to convince decision makers, who have probably seen several solutions already, he has to have deep insight into and broad understanding of the industry offerings, as well as what may or may not be good for the customer.

3. Storytelling—Along with knowledge, the effecter should also possess powerful storytelling skills to keep the prospect interested and instill the value proposition in the prospect's mind. Effecters should be personable and engage with people easily.

4. Closing—The effecter has to break the whole buying process into logical steps, and help map the buying decision for prospects in order to effect the closing (or product finalizing).

5. Sales/Product strategy—Effecters in service industries have a revenue target, and they have to plan the sales strategy. Effecters in product companies have

a shared top-line and bottom-line responsibility and so they are accountable for establishing a product roadmap and executing as per the roadmap. With inputs from educators, enablers and engagers, the effecters work the approach for the whole team.

6. Finance management—The effecter has to ensure that he is not overspending on any of the planned activities toward the deal closures and product development. He also periodically checks the effectiveness of brand building exercise, advertisements and promotions.

CHAPTER SUMMARY

The Educate phase interactions helped us identify the engaging zone between the entrepreneur and the customer. The Enable phase took the understanding of customers' product needs, and helped the entrepreneur build the engaging zone. An engaging zone as we saw in the last chapter is a product specification range (around price, product features, delivery methods, among other parameters), where the product parameters brought value to the customer, and were cost effective (and product-strategy-wise reasonable) to develop for the entrepreneur.

Effect can be a sale, a deal closure, or an approval from a prospect—all essentially drawing the prospective customer into the Engaging zone. The Effect phase is about getting the customer to commit to the product or service. The effecter does not wait for an opportunity but creates it at the earliest moment he can. He does not worry about hustle or hassle. Some of the strengths that the effecter uses include his agility, his subject matter expertise, his storytelling, his closing skills, his sales strategy, and his ability to manage the budget and finances. The effecter's pitches most often target the stem (or the survival instinct). For complex services, he works closely with prospects and helps them sell to their supervisors.

The effecter team works on strategic activities around forecasting, team building, and coaching. The effecter team also has an equally significant number of tactical tasks—picking the right candidates, building trust, mapping buying decisions, and closing.

For forecasting, the effecter considers a variety of factors affecting sales including economic cycles, changing customer behavior, competition from unforeseen quarters, and increases in the cost of goods. A good forecast saves the entrepreneurial business from problems with too much or too little inventory, changing competition, rising costs, and shifting customer priorities. An effecter also knows how important partnerships are, particularly if the project needs competencies and skills outside the realm of the entrepreneur's. A lot of firms have only a few effecters and their growth stalls, if their effecters get stretched. Hence, there is need of knowledge redundancy as a disaster recovery mechanism. Effecters focus on team collaboration and also on transferring some of the ideas, contacts and strategies to new effecters.

Effecters are on the constant lookout for new product functionalities, and sales opportunities. Add to that, producing and distributing a product may not always be cost effective enough. Even the fact that other products exist in the market and which can serve somewhat the same purpose can deter these effecters.

Effecters look into the key traits of prospect groups and see what would make them buy their product/service. Using attributes and filters, effecters look closely at where to place prospects in the perceived likelihood buckets (high or low) of getting into the engaging zone. Effecters gather educator's data, enabler's analytics and engager's recent interactions to see how much the missing gap means to the prospective customers and how much the prospects are losing in terms of money, image and time, with status quo conditions.

Effecters improvise and experiment with new ideas, remain flexible to the end goal, and then capture the successes in a model and replicate it as there is no assurance from interested prospects that they will get engaged for the long term. The improvising is done by changing parameters of the product or service to make them more amicable to the customer's needs. The central theme again is to get the customers into the engaging zone or the zone, identified by educators and built by enablers.

Figure 4.4 Your Moving Services, Inc.

Case Study—Your Moving Services, Inc.

While you were moving into the first apartment after college, the whole move was orchestrated before your eyes through the process of locating a mover that fitted your budget. The experience stayed with you as you began your entrepreneurial explorations and finally you thought there was a business you could start. There was not much infrastructure cost to set up (perhaps a few trucks), not many players in the market, and no major regulatory requirements. You had wondered if it could scale multiple geographies and different segments (students and then corporate moves). Then you got busy at work—working endlessly on reports. Ten years down the road, and after working at a few companies, the entrepreneurial bug bit you.

The first thing you did was identifying the market size and making a decision whether it was something worth venturing into. You divided the city into a grid. You researched the number of moves that happen in each of these areas every year, based on the number of households, demographics, colleges and offices in the area, commuters, train stations, real estate taxes, rental rates, and historical data for five years among other parameters. You came up with a projected number for the next year. For each grid you looked at the number of moving firms and put a supplier power to them based on their size, presence, and historical numbers. You got a good understanding of the geographic areas and demographic segments where you identified an unmet need.

But what happens if none of the prospects know you? Your journey through Four E framework just started.

You started by visiting colleges. You knew the administration at your college, and as an alumnus you reached out to the current students and spoke about how you would give them a 25 percent discount when they decide to use your services. You saw some leads within a week after the announcement. You also came across referrals, but again student moves are seasonal. So, you decided to build a more stable stream of work. You put your promotion in the local couponing magazine. In addition, you approached PR firms for some press releases.

Again, your alumni network helped. You approached companies with your press releases and took print outs of reviews and testimonials with you when you went to meet with the corporate honchos. What effecter tools should you use to make the deal sweet for them and sweeter for you? Remember you have to get them to an engaging zone.

For identifying the engaging zone, you should have already worked on your value proposition. What did you want to engage the customer with? An affordable moving service, a fast and safe moving service or a high-quality scratch-free guaranteed move?

Let us say you were offering the high-quality scratch-free guaranteed move. Can you execute that? What would you need to successfully engage the customers? Perhaps, bonded lifters and movers with several years of experience.

(Continued)

(Continued)

Can you afford them? If you were to employ a few of these moving stars you would have to pay them well. Or perhaps give them a percentage of what you made with every move, so that they felt partners in the process and were incentivized to do a really great job every time.

Alternatively, you could be the low-price king. For that, you had to recruit minimum wage employees and train them. There may be a few bad moves (unintended pun), initially, but ultimately it may be successful. But the risk is that a few bad moves can shatter your dreams.

Based on these calculations, you can build the engaging zone. You determined the right service, the pricing, accessibility, promotions, team, tools and even the potential start of partnerships.

Now is the time to do more strategic effecting. Would teaming with a rental truck service be considered a good idea? Also, how would you like to try coast to coast moves? Would you consider teaming with XYZ Van Lines for that? And how would that teaming change your engaging zone with the corporate honchos you were talking to earlier?

Initially, XYZ Van Lines did not want to collaborate. How would you establish trust? Would you talk about your success stories? Would it make sense to point at some lessons learned from your past flaws? Even if XYZ Van Lines does not come through you may want to talk to other similar outfits.

Your bargaining chip is your relationships. As it is a dog-eat-dog world, XYZ Van Lines can actually go talk directly to the corporate honchos? How would you prevent that from happening?

Among all this, you were also pursuing a selling angle with residents of the areas that were not being served by some of your direct competitors. So you started hunting for consumers with sponsorship of local events, fliers with promotions, and at other places. You kept yourself open to questions from prospective customers. You could even recommend other ways to relocate as a service to build relationships and generate positive word. Openness can build trust and help in closing more deals.

Some of these answers will be better answered in the next chapter but the effect aspect is all about getting the customers to commit to the product. The effect phase focuses on ensuring that both the customer and the entrepreneur get the value they are comfortable with. If for some reason either or both parties do not think they are getting the value, effecters identify how changes in product or service parameters can help the value be brought back in the relationship. The next chapter will talk about ways to sustain these values for the long term.

5

ENGAGE PHASE

The terms "sales" and "marketing" are still used interchangeably in many entrepreneurial firms. It was traditionally assumed that anyone in sales dedicated a great deal of time in identifying prospects and developing new opportunities. However, as these small businesses grew, specializations rose, and sales and marketing became not only two different departments but two separate islands. Most sales organizations were too busy taking orders and ignored seeking new business and marketing for it. Over time, this situation led to the creation of "farmers" for nurturing the relationships with existing customers.

With increasing competition and shrinking customer pools, the focus changed from just nurturing to just seeking new customers. That happened when "hunters" came in, and all of a sudden the industry started focusing on only new business and ignored the retention of existing customers. The more successful entrepreneurial firms, however, did not leave the existing customers: They kept them engaged or they kept them in the engaging zone, ensuring that the entrepreneur as well as customers still got value out of that relationship. The engage phase is where we talk about engaging the customer for the long term.

There is a huge difference between closing one deal with a customer and the total revenue the same customer gives you over the lifetime of its business relationship with you. The lifetime revenue from a customer heavily depends on the relationship (and the connection) between you and that customer. Which is where you have to be a careful judge of how much you are willing to spend every year, so that the net revenue from this customer far out-runs the cost of keeping this bond strong.

When Frank Adams started at Figaro X Ray as an accounts manager, he had asked Hugh, the sales chief, some questions in an email:

1. Do the customers know us well? Do they trust us?
2. How many key influencers do we know at the customer's decision-making team?
3. Are influencers leaning toward competing products/services? What are those competing products?
4. Any plans of positively influencing these influencers to like our product better?
5. Do price increases/changes need to be negotiated?
6. Are upselling and cross-selling possible?
7. Does a referral process work for getting new clients?
8. Do we have subject-matter experts that can help new (or unvisited) unmet needs of our customers?

Hugh could respond to only a few of these questions as he needed more data and Figaro did not have any tools of engagement back then. That was how Frank had made a strong business case for implementing a CRM system at Figaro within a year of joining the firm.

On an average a business loses around 20 percent of its customers annually simply by failing to attend to

Figure 5.1 Engage

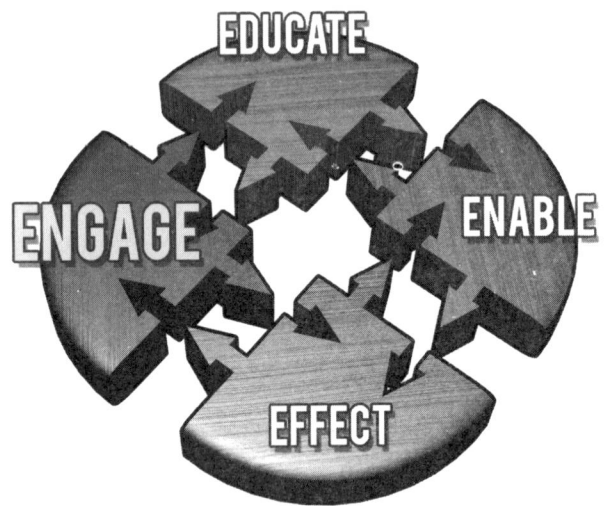

customer relationships. With rising customer acquisition costs, these small businesses' inability to retain their clients is immediately reflected in their accounting books. Acquiring new customers can cost almost six times more than retaining existing customers.

Now you may be doing an excellent service in keeping your customers happy. And existing customers leaving may not always be due to their dissatisfaction with the service or the product. They may leave to try out another product or they are just in the market for another need and chance upon a product that serves multiple needs.

As a result, entrepreneurial firms have to innovate. They also have to engage these customers with other services/products and keep them loyal. Talking about loyalty, I have divided the customers or the influencers into four groups, based on their levels of loyalty—I refer to the most loyal as "the evangelists", the second in the hierarchy being "the loyal", the third are what I call the indifferent, and the fourth are "the deterred".

Engagers strive to take the indifferent customers and make them evangelists. And at the same time, identify what would provide more clarity to the deterred customers. The deterred customers are those that are either in love with a competing company's product/service or they are not in full agreement with how your company has been delivering or engaging lately.

Most of the time, however, the customer is not of any one type. Instead, they are a mix of different types of influencers at the customer site—some evangelists or loyal while others either indifferent or deterred. The engager's task then becomes to identify these influencers, categorize them into corresponding buckets, and carry out engaging tasks. All these can be accomplished through tools of engagement, which we will read about in a later section.

Figure 5.2 Influencer Categories

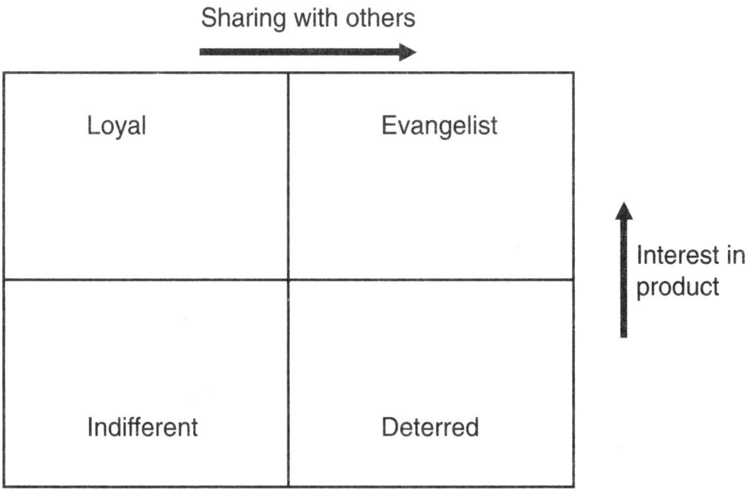

WHY DO EVANGELISTS CARE?

Thanks to social media, a large majority of people love to talk about themselves—products they use, vehicles they drive, services they use, and so on. The driver to all this talking-about-self is the idea of being more interesting and socially more acceptable. These desires can be tapped into.

1. These customers believe that "In the know" factor makes them sound more interesting. They want to be the stars in the groups—social events or industry forums. To achieve this they update themselves about things happening around. They are also on the lookout for new devices and products to try and to let the world know about, as their discoveries will make them look cool.

2. Consumers also like "commonality" around the use of an item or knowledge of a subject. They like to talk to others who use similar products or have similar interests. If there is anyone who asks for a recommendation or reference, this ability to give advice heightens their self-importance and general utility.

Customer engagement can be more effective if you can get your product into your customers' "in the know" list of products and have them build a "commonality of use" net around them where they refer others to your product. Let us start that process by listening first.

LISTENING AND EXECUTING

Whereas effecting has a component of spontaneity, engaging is more orchestrated, planned, and directed. More control lies in engaging, and engagers deal with a known audience to reach out to. In highly specialized professional services, effecters aim to be trusted advisors and consultants, while engagers want to keep a steady flow of business by remaining in the good books of the influencers. Engagers also have accountability for fulfilling and project managing the orders. The moment a purchase order floats in or the customer signs a contract, the engagers start the fulfilling action steps. The engagers keep close contact with the customer during the execution, and customize the offering to better cater to customer needs and increase the loyalty of their customers. The goal is to keep customers happy and wanting more.

Engaging entrepreneurs that see the biggest gains are those that listen to their customers. The idea is not to just listen to customers but to go to the root cause of their concerns and apply solutions where appropriate. Searching for these improvement possibilities is the first step to getting customers happy and wanting more. The next step is to measure these objectives against established standards/ benchmarks and see where any inconsistencies are more pronounced. Finally, it is necessary to prioritize these steps based on the need of improvement in critical functions to help the client grow revenue-wise (improve top-line), or incorporate better saving strategies (improve bottom-line).

The entrepreneur listens to the customer in each phase, improving incrementally upon the solution for resolving pain points. During *educate*, the entrepreneur gathers an overview of customers' pain points and what they value. During *enable*, the entrepreneur goes into more specifics and identifies what the product/service parameters should be so that customers could remove the pain.

During *effect*, the entrepreneur listens to customers to plan what it would take to have them be engaged to the entrepreneur's product. And in *engage*, the entrepreneur goes even deeper and ensures that customers who choose his product are successful in accomplishing what they want to.

With changing technology (increasing mobile app use, social media, and so on), rising incomes in developing countries and perspective and mindset differences between generations, the consumer is getting exposed to new products. With the continuously changing economic environment and consumer preferences, entrepreneurs are willing to cater to these changing needs of the consumers. This change can also necessitate geographic expansion and subsequently the firm learns the local culture in new geographies in order to engage prospects better. Some companies adapt quickly to such changes by making a platform of standard base product and then configuring functionalities to suit the interests, as opposed to building a custom product for every new customer segment.

When GXXView took its offerings to market, it was a small company working on custom products for its customers. However, as it saw a pattern of needs that were common across its customer base, it pivoted its business model to move into configuring as opposed to customizing. That is when they started building a platform with levers to configure it. The standard product would resolve the most common pain points and then the company would further configure the product to address any client specific needs.

Suzanne from Kabob Times also started small and customized the food as per the need of customers. However, as she gained more loyal customers, she established a standard menu and only served those items that were on her menu with minimal change.

Figaro's team took this standardization step even further with simple steps, and built modules for:

- Making planning easy for Figaro's customers.
- Making parts and applications configurable so that customers could do some of the design-to-fit work themselves.
- Helping customers with access to important data points so that customers could do their own analysis.

Much centered on Figaro's listening to their customers and adding purpose to act suitably on those needs, thus converting active listening into active execution.

Similarly, as GXXview started its product development, the needs of the customer evolved, and GXXview kept adding iteratively to the finished product until the customer got what they wanted (and perhaps much more). Subsequently, this idea was commercialized and up-sold to other prospects as well. That's how GXXView effectually engaged its customers by listening to them and working with them.

PROVIDING LONG-TERM SOLUTIONS

Organizations are replacing existing solutions that point to a single pain point with end-to-end solutions. This keeps accountabilities with one vendor firm and critical problems get resolved faster (unlike the traditional way where service level agreements defined the speed of resolution on a defined portfolio of related systems). It also enables the business to make strategic business decisions.

ABC Engineering had to work with other vendors of the customer, when the company started working on a managed services' contract for one of its customers. Separate vendors had their own service-level agreements, thus causing bottlenecks in application support, particularly during application outages (when applications or their hardware crashed). ABC Engineering took a step back to look at the vendor organization and subsequently conducted a study. It found that the customer reduced dependency on multiple vendors for the same outcome and brought about significant cost savings and faster problem solving when one firm managed the maintenance function end-to-end.

ABC Engineering shared these findings with CIO, and as per the study outcome, recommended making changes to the application portfolio support program. The CIO loved what was recommended. ABC Engineering lost some work and gained some others, but it had already made a deep impact and the leaders at the customer saw how they could benefit by engaging ABC Engineering in long-term strategic planning work.

INTEGRATING THE CUSTOMER ENTERPRISE

As we saw earlier, GXXview's mobile product played a great role in differentiation. The mobile application helped the utility customer become more efficient as they could use their mobile device conveniently from anywhere and get latest updates on outstanding orders as well as work on open work orders, based on pre-programmed decisions and criteria. Engaging customers by keeping them apprised all the time with such an application was invaluable.

ABC Engineering also built a similar reporting dash-board to help customers see the open support tickets, and the estimated time to resolve those elements. That went a long way in engaging their customers.

***

Every large customer complains about "islands of information" or groups working in isolation. Customers suffer as a result of fragmented structures. Alignment of these groups is possible by understanding the workflows of each department. The engager goes through workflows and identifies where the points of failure are. Subsequently, he makes recommendations to close those gaps (through better processes, more automation, implementing an application that does the same work, or by outsourcing the work to a third party). An engager also acts as a change manager and manages expectations after a change.

CUSTOMER RETENTION THROUGH COMMUNICATION

The easiest way to grow your business is to not lose your customers. The cost of losing customers is staggering, but few businesses truly understand the implications.

Let us say there are two companies: Every year one retains 80 percent of its customers, the other 50 percent. If both of them add 50 percent new customers per year, the first will have a 30 percent net growth in customers per year, while the other will have none. Over a few years, the first firm will double and then triple, while the second will remain the same. The second one is essentially adding, and losing the same number. Now, take the same rationale and think about companies that lose a bigger percentage than they acquire. Those companies could be in their path of shutting down their operations, unless they have changed their model and designed products where they are better off having a few customers.

Jeff Kahn, the retail businessman, measured the satisfaction of customers by looking at how customer expectations were managed, and how loyal the customers became during the sales and the fulfilling process. Some of his engagers practiced gold plating by going that extra mile in making sure the customers were getting everything they asked for and more. And that was good as long as the customer appreciated that extra effort the engagers put. Jeff observed, however, that turning these customers into evangelists required the engagers to identify other potential pains of the customer and provide solutions to these customers—solutions that these evangelists wanted others to have, as that would engender commonality around use of that solution.

***

GXXView also built and maintained relationships by communicating through a series of letters, emails, events, phone calls, and newsletters even after they sold them their entire roster of products/services. The goal was to make them evangelists and not just satisfied customers.

Engagers at Figaro X Ray sent surveys to customers to see how they liked the experience, and if they had any feedback. Customers responded positively by saying that they felt valued, and important. Figaro also reached out and re-activated old customers who were once with them and knew their product well. Figaro knew that these dormant leads did not need a lot of work to bring back to the fold to increase sales. Connecting, and sending them emails about their new products resulted in some new deals in a matter of months. They understood that satisfied customers not only buy more, they become repeat or loyal customers. Moreover, some loyal customers continually tell others how well they were treated and become evangelists for the firm.

MANAGING DELIVERY

Delivery is at the heart of engaging customers, particularly when it comes to providing services. This is even truer now as support department activities are being increasingly outsourced at mid-sized to large organizations. An entrepreneurial firm getting into a service delivery contract with a large organization has to engage the company by first understanding the culture, the process workflows, the stakeholders, and also the strategic objectives of the organizations.

Imagine you have a water boiler that boils water very efficiently. If a problem arises with the piping (a break in piping or leakage of water somewhere), the hot water does not make it to the bathroom. Ultimately, you receive a fairly fat bill without even getting hot water. In essence, that is what happens when companies buy services and products and do not get engaged in the right manner. Managing company-wide adoption is essential for effectively engaging. More important, however, is the adoption course, and governance of the change management process to ensure that the change has positively impacted the existing workflows.

When a municipal client in California first bought the GXXView service, the leadership team was not in complete alignment with the application use, and some leaders were even skeptical of the need. The public works department thought the service was useful, but the planning department believed it was just an addition to the large number of tools they already had. The GXXView team had to engage all the stakeholders and help each of them understand where in their workflow the product would help.

For the public works department, the product would show the location of the sewer mains while for the planning group it would enable them to work on urban development plans with demographic information and electronic maps. Subsequently, the organization had to train personnel from all departments so that they could carry out their work most effectively. The GXXView team also built key performance indicator metrics to promote transparency among the different teams. The whole initiative not only helped employees benefit from the tool, but also made them aware of the strategic objectives of their groups and the organization as well.

ENGAGING WITH CHANGE MANAGEMENT

Change is always challenging, particularly when users question why there is an altered way of doing things from how they were always done. New product rollouts and launches are important times to engage the customer in a change.

Take the case of vending machines. From the first vending machines in the US in the late 19th century that sold gums, vending machines now have undergone several rounds of improvement. Each of these improvements were implemented to keep customers more engaged in terms of new products, new payment options, and overall experience. Vending machines now are smart, so much so that these machines can integrate data analytics and can remotely manage inventory, sales and even refilling. In effect, customers have a better product experience and are kept engaged.

Let us consider another example. In one of ABC Engineering's engagements, the engaging team there had to make a change to the existing operating system (move users from an older operating system to a newer one). It involved working through 2,000 computer applications that employees (users) were using. Some of the steps they carried out to build more engagement included:

Communication of Change

The ABC team communicated not only the fact that they were changing the environment, but that the new environment came with better tooling, higher security, and more vendor support. ABC informed them much in advance of the benefits of the new environment and kept them informed all throughout the rollout. ABC quickly learned that engaging all customers by letting them ask questions was key to making them partners in the process. As the first wave of users migrated into the new environment, ABC team asked them to give their feedback and leveraged those lessons learned to provide an even better experience to the subsequent groups. Thus, incrementally, improving their engagement style.

Benefit Realization

ABC team had prepared a detailed schedule and included an overview of "where the migrations were" section in the communication. That was where the ABC team assessed the metrics to measure the success of the rollout, as well as identified the benefits to ensure that the implementation was following the plan. As the ABC team progressed by migrating more users each week, they realized more benefits for the organization. They also got evangelists within the migrated groups, who engaged the remaining users better.

Training and Engagement Metrics

With rollouts come changed processes, new interfaces and frustration. To minimize the negative impact and stress, it was important to train users in the new environment. The training was done face-to-face as well as through virtual set up. The documentation informed users of the new process and environment, and also contained instructions on the key changes that were made in the old interface and additions in the new one. The ABC team took some of the super-users and trained them first (through "train the trainer" sessions) and that helped them build evangelists and disseminate knowledge.

The ABC team revisited the issues and key success factors to ascertain how close the execution was to the team's benchmark. The ABC team also gathered inputs from time to time to see how the strategic changes were coming into play.

Clearly, the people-side and the change-management tasks were more challenging than the technological constraints that different applications bore. As ABC identified that early in the project, the engaging zone was built at the outset. From there, the delivery process ensured that every user got engaged before getting migrated and remained engaged and satisfied even after that.

RULES AND TOOLS OF ENGAGEMENT

A lot can be achieved with the help of big data and predictive analysis. However, simple rules and tools can do some of the heavy lifting too as the key is to select a good mix of indicators. It is necessary, too, to look at the quality of opportunities that are won. How much margin is the firm making? Has the offering been gold plated so much that the firm is losing its shirt on this customer? Is this just a one-time buy or there is a future with the customer? What kind of scope and timelines were agreed upon? Were the timelines and scope too aggressive? Many of these questions are answerable if the analysis rules and tools are right.

Rules of Engagement

When it comes to the rules of engagement, one of the most important things for the chief engager to look at is metrics that address arriving at better sales results or forecasts:

- where are we and why;
- where are we falling behind; and
- how can we improve.

At GXXView, all opportunities were recorded and a probability percentage was assigned to each opportunity. The sales funnel was a composite of probable opportunities. GXXView played with the levers to increase sales efficiency by:

1. Increasing the probability, and decreasing the decision length: Besides the account's interest and the salesperson's effectiveness, three other parameters usually influence sales—opportunity value, timing and probability. Opportunity value was a finite and stable value in most cases. Engagers shared with prospects how important the small window for getting all the moving parts lined up was. In order to shorten the decision timeframe, the engagers bundled projects as well as gave discounts to customers for such bundles.

   The engagers also carefully identified probability and assessed whether or not the probability was increasing with time. If the probability was very low, they dug deeper to identify the possibility of raising that. Again, engagers were invaluable in identifying what interested the customers most. As the closing probabilities rose and got to a certain percentage, effecters and senior leadership team were involved to take that to a close.

2. Tracking different revenue levers: GXXview also had a service arm that used to convert engineering map data for these agencies. Data conversion was a capital intensive task, and most of the time the application sale was a minor sale compared to the data conversion revenues. However data conversion was a one-time sale, whereas hosting an application was a recurring revenue source.

   In addition to the different lines of businesses, GXXView was in the process of expanding from the

West Coast to the East Coast and signed some early adopters there for these services. GXXView could track sales opportunities by customers (new, existing, or prospect), by lines of business (products or services), by geography (NY, NJ CA or OR) by channels (sales team or partners) and identify how revenues were impacted if the levers were tweaked.

3. Looking at the cost of sales: Identifying the cost of sales can help the entrepreneur understand the efficiency of the sales team. Sales costs include salaries, administrative, support and general expenses for the sales team. The ratio of the cost to the revenues helped GXXView compare the sales teams in different lines of business, separate geographies, and sales channels. The team that had the lowest cost for every dollar in sales was the team that was studied and followed so that the firm can use those processes across other groups. The inherent disadvantages associated with geographies, customer groups, among others were also considered while deriving the cost of sales.

Tools of Engagement

Perhaps the most important utility these days in managing customer relationships is a group of tools referred to as the CRM system, used for sales and support services by several organizations. CRM evolved from multiple sources, but primarily from contact management systems.

What used to be a rolodex sitting on an office desk became an electronic customer and contact management system for searching accounts, reporting opportunities, and following engagement trends. With the advent of computer interface, tracking salespeople and trending sales opportunities became simple. Subsequent to that, a use case to support customer issues also got included in CRM systems. There, the Engager used CRM for recording the complaint and following up with the users. This is similar to how work orders are generated and a problem solver gets assigned to it. The CRM system therefore doubles up as knowledge management system as well as an issue-resolution information base for these customers.

The commercial off-the-shelf CRM systems integrate these two areas of tracking sales and support issues into a single system. Running algorithms on this information to identify and trend the customer's unmet needs can define an engagement strategy that matches what customers need in terms of products and services. Such a system helps prioritize the marketing dollars and does away with wasteful time/resource spending with prospects. It also makes coordination easy for teams involved in sales, marketing, call centers and retail outlets.

However, a system of this sort should not lead to an over ambitious spending for an engager. According to CSO Insights' 2006 Sales Performance Optimization study, less than 40 percent of 1,275 participating companies had end-user adoption rates above 90 percent.

Besides support and training on CRM systems, a lot depends on user-friendliness in applications as well as the combination of features one selects to make the users more effective and efficient.

Source: http://www.destinationcrm.com/Articles/ Columns-Departments/Reality-Check/Demystifying- CRM-Adoption-Rates-42496.aspx (Accessed on November 3, 2015).

Can a company not do all this with MS Excel or in traditional ways, particularly if the firm has only a few major customers, and the line of business does not call for regular update meetings with the customer?

Yes it can.

CRM data from the past and from disparate sources can, however, be used by the educating, enabling, effecting and engaging groups to define engaging zone and plan strategic moves beyond tactical changes. But, a CRM implementation is successful and effective only when the entrepreneur clearly defines the benefits, and phases the whole implementation by putting checkpoints and gates at important milestones to identify whether the system is fulfilling every need foreseen.

As a lot of CRM applications are similar regarding functionalities, the one most closely aligned with the business and which is most cost effective will be what the engagement team chooses. Dashboards depicting the current state of what is in the pipeline and what are the key support risks are useful. Also, the way the CRM can be integrated with other systems (beyond sales, support and invoicing) is another vital aspect that should be considered when deciding on one.

CRMs also leverage social media to build up customer relationships. Some CRM systems even integrate social media sites to track and communicate with customers in order to understand their experiences with a product.

REVISITING YOUR BUSINESS PURPOSE

Why are you in the business? What is it that you promised? With today's dynamic business environment, some of the customer needs may have changed and the market may have other products taking better care of the pain. Or perhaps you did not keep up with what you promised. Apply a different lens to see whether the promise you made to your customers still holds true. The more aligned your philosophy today is with the original one, the more engaged customers will be.

According to a study by the Gallup Group, customers engage more with a brand when they find the service to be responsive. Allowing customer ideas to be incorporated in the service/products gives the customer a feeling of ownership in the product, and subsequently they become evangelists of the product and promote the product in their social circle.

The design and serviceability of your product or service must also be aligned with what your customers want. If customers do not like your selling process, they will never buy from you again let alone referring their friends to you. Integrity is also reflected in how you handle detailed as well as big-picture factors. You will certainly retain customers if you are open and honest with them.

Price and place are important in getting new customers, but the more important thing is to keep customers engaged. According to the 2014 Gallup hospitality industry study, hotels would do better if they remove amenities that do not bring value to customers, and instead recruited and developed employees to engage customers and reap significantly higher share of spends from these loyal customers.

Source: http://www.gallup.com/businessjournal/175568/economy-luxury-matters-hotel-guests.aspx (Accessed on November 3, 2015).

Figure 5.3 Customer Relationship and Contact Management

ENGAGER CHARACTERISTICS

For an entrepreneurial firm, the engagers are the level-headed individuals who understand the big picture and work on long-term returns. As Engagers are responsible for strengthening the relationships with existing customers, and getting more business out of them, they find themselves in account management or farming roles. With today's changes in the marketplace, the modern engager has a much more important role to play in the sales process—more than just working a few accounts for more business.

The engager's key goal is to understand how to keep creating value for customers, and delivering solutions efficiently.

In the All-hands meeting every month, when the Figaro X-Ray sales team met, Hugh started by sharing some of the key opportunities he had closed and also what he was hopeful of closing. He used to get deep into methodologies and experiences which limited the time for others to speak. He was under the gun back then. However, in the last two years, Frank had been gaining substantially more spotlight. Perhaps now that the company had established some stable customers, they were eager to provide more devices or services to the customers.

Figaro's sales team head did not define roles in the best possible way. Hugh wanted Frank to go to each of the customers that Hugh got and get more business. Frank always wanted to grow Figaro from a mom-and-pop shop to a larger and more sustainable firm. Frank had initiated a farming exercise as he knew that selling new customers a few machines and holding onto these customers for future services are two completely different strategies. In order to retain customers, the company needed to prove that it was capable of delivering and customizing the orders as per the customer's needs.

This is when Frank put together a list of skills that he valued and were important for all engagers:

1. Engagers should have strong foresight. Good engagers are able to think of the problems before encountering them and resolve them before they jeopardize deadlines or budgets and become huge obstacles. Engagers, are the delivery or project managers, who should have their attention focused on the scope, schedule, budget, resources, and quality constraints.

2. Engagers can bring array in chaotic environments. Handovers from effecters to engagers are typically not always clean. Annoyed and anxious customers are what they get to see first in most cases. A good engager cuts through all the noise, re-prioritizes everything, revisits the issues, creates permanent solutions, and then keeps it that way. The outcome of all this? Evangelists in customers.

3. Engagers should be great leaders and communicators. Engagers interact with the customers, their stakeholder teams and sponsors. To influence those, who have no answerability to the engager is always a challenge. Communication and leading effectively comes into play as the engager needs to develop trust with the stakeholders about issues, risks and possible changes in scope, schedule, and budgets.

4. Engagers should prioritize carefully with attention to time, and resource management, as they deliver critical projects. It is essential to keep the stakeholders and team members informed and make them partners in the process.

BACK TO EDUCATE

For the customer to remain engaged and be in the engaging zone, the entrepreneur keeps the value that both parties are getting out of the relationship in mind. This cycle of Educate-Enable-Effect-Engage continues with the engaged customer. With the engaged customer, educators identify other unmet needs and new priorities. To bring more value, the educators also reveal some of the new products the entrepreneurial firm is working on. Subsequently, enablers and effecters play into the relationship as well not to monetize this transactional opportunity but to increase the lifetime value of these customers by keeping them in the engaging zone.

CHAPTER SUMMARY

The Educate, Enable, and Effect Phase interactions helped us identify the engaging zone boundaries, build the engaging zone with the parameters identified, and then draw the prospect customer into the engaging zone. Engage phase is about keeping the customer within the engaging zone by constantly creating value for the customer. Much centers on listening to customers so as to act suitably on those, and converting active listening into active execution to keep delivering value.

Organizations are replacing existing legacy solutions with end-to-end solutions, so the same vendor now can be accountable for a whole function. Customers also suffer as a result of fragmented structures. Alignment of these groups is possible by adroit engagers. Having enterprise-wide systems and more accountability in processes, analytics and controls to manage possible failures go a long way in keeping customers engaged and informed all the time.

We also saw that the easiest way to grow your business is to not lose your customers. The cost of losing customers is staggering, but few businesses truly understand the implications. Customers also tend to place importance on the values of the company, so the philosophy today should not be too different from what it was when the entrepreneur started.

Delivery is at the heart of engaging customers. An entrepreneurial firm getting into a service delivery contract with a large organization has to engage it by understanding the culture, the process workflows, the frameworks used, and the strategic objectives of the organization.

Users at customer-organizations question as to why there is an altered way of doing things from how they were always done. New product rollouts and launches are important times to engage these users and customers, and to explain the benefits of the change to the business.

Benefits get realized sooner with more engagement. Even reaching out and re-activating old customers to bring back to the fold to increase sales is one area that does not need a lot of work.

Managing relationships with old, existing, and prospective customers can be done through a CRM system, used for sales and support services by several organizations. Dynamically tracking salespeople and trending sales have become convenient with such systems. There is also a support aspect of CRM for helping the users with issues.

Engagers have strong foresight; they are practical and open. Engagers interact with the customers, their stakeholder teams and sponsors. Prioritization, time and

Figure 5.4 Your Staffing Company

resource management are all important strengths of the engager to keep the engagement on track and make the engagement successful.

Case Study—Your Staffing Company, Inc.

While you were looking for a job, you might have wondered whether it was a good idea to start a staffing firm. No upfront cost to set up and no major infrastructure costs. All you needed were people who were familiar with the business. You could work a pay schedule so that your staff could be paid after you get paid. For that you had to shorten receivables, and stretch your payables.

You might have toyed with the idea of a consulting firm. There was some effort in overcoming the catch 22 quandary. You struggled with the thoughts of how do you hire consultants, who could get you top dollars for their work? How do you establish relationships with customers who could trust you, and pay top dollars? Why would consultants need you if they could directly strike a deal with these companies? What kind of contract do you have to establish with these companies (your customers) and with the consultants. Did you want to employ these consultants or just have a contractual relationship as long as they were billable? Would you focus on management consulting or IT strategy consulting? Would it be easier to start with augmenting support staff for companies? Or would it make more sense to work with temporary staff first and then get into more complex aspects?

Then you started thinking about handyman services. Dealing with consumers directly was less hassle, but then lining up engagements was too much work. Margins were low, hours stretched into the weekend, and news of one bad work traveled faster than the good reputation built over numerous years.

You also thought about other staffing ideas—modeling agency and even contract janitorial services. However, the risks and costs in all these areas, at least for the first few years, were significantly more than the benefits.

(*Continued*)

(Continued)

You settled on temporary staffing services. After educating yourself about market conditions, you worked on enabling aspects, pricing your services, identifying the scope of your services, selecting your locations, preparing your brochures and promotional material. Then you started effecting by going through a list of prospective customers, calling them, and getting meetings scheduled. At these meetings you talked about your value proposition—how you differentiated yourself from others by offering the value that customers needed at a low price.

But ask yourself: what other offerings could help you differentiate yourself from your competitors?

In the first six months, you got four companies signing up for your services and had 24 temps working at their organizations. As you started engaging them, you listened to their other pains and shared how you thought you could solve their problems. You acted on those. You also talked how you solved problems at other places (using some of the best practices such as making the processes transparent). You also recommended tools for getting reports faster.

How did you identify what the best practices were in your portfolio of clients?

Three months later, you revisited your mission. You also organized a small user group meeting to talk to your customers. Were you following the same vision that you started with? Has the market changed? Do you need more standards for taking your game a notch higher? How did you manage your delivery? Did you have any knowledge management process, so that all you learned about customers could stay within the company?

As you grew organically, you built a stronger effecting team that took some of these case studies to your prospect customers. You also had account managers, who engaged the existing customers. In order to manage all these leads, you subscribed to a cloud-based CRM tool that all the engagers and effecters could use and track the leads. What metrics would you look at more often to gauge customer's increasing interest?

At this point in time as you had some very loyal customers, did you contemplate getting into high-end consulting? Or did you want to stay in the same space and expand geographically? Did you want a product to go along with your services to bring about more value and differentiation in your services? At what point did you connect with educators to transfer your knowledge of customer pain points as well as understand some of the new offerings?

As you grow through this cycle of Educate-Enable-Effect-Engage, you will realize that it is a process of continuous improvement. You will also come across loyal customers who have your utmost attention but are always looking elsewhere for something that fits their agenda. It is a good idea to periodically rank your customers in a four-box matrix—to identify the evangelists, the loyal customers, and the difficult

(*Continued*)

(Continued)

customers. It is better to let go of the difficult customers, who become a cost rather than a benefit. Some customers may also become transferors of your proprietary information to your competitors. As there is negative value in keeping such customers, it is better to get them out of your engaging zone as soon as you identify them.

CONCLUSION

From our chapters we saw how important it is to have a customer before selling a product. A Four E framework helps in creating the engaging zone and engaging the customer therein. The Four E framework is a lot about situational leadership and immersing oneself into an engagement role. It is also about ensuring that the customer is getting value from the relationship. That engagement enables a prototype to become a minimum viable product and further evolve to get to MVP.

A large majority of entrepreneurs are so passionate about their innovations that they get distracted and as a result they burn a significant portion of the budget on bells and whistles or functions that their customers do not want. The feedback loop ensures rich bidirectional flow of information in all the engagement phases during this evolution so that the customer is identified and engaged even before the product is launched.

Let us go back to the product lifecycle to see how the Four E framework keeps the customer engaged through the product lifecycle. Educators can help the introduction phase of the product lifecycle, as that is when the entrepreneurial firm seeks ideas as well as builds product awareness. Enablers expand the market and enable more and more people to start using the product, during the growth phase of the product lifecycle.

When a product reaches its maturity phase, the effecters assess the value the product brings to the customer and decide the proper mix of marketing dollars to lend the greatest profits. When the product is in its decline phase, there is a gradual disinterest in the product. The engagers there keep the customers in the engaging zone and help them with other products (or better version of the same product) through the engaged relationship, thus increasing the lifetime value of the customers.

The customer-engaging entrepreneur needs to take value creation for customers to new horizons, through better procedures, and build competencies to support that. It requires the entrepreneur to revisit his entire way of conducting business and identify the engaging zone. It would also help him to keep looking for opportunities in adjacent categories; or new value pockets in existing competencies.

Enablers can help build efficiency to deliver the right product efficiently in a way the customer wants. Educators can help identify insights about customers that in turn drive marketing and sales decisions. Effecters can help extend necessary competencies to increase value for customers. Engagers can use these newly developed competencies to improve how customers are served and how they get the best possible experience, across all product lines and services.

All these facets, when combined effectively, within the entrepreneurial firm can acquire new customers and retain them in the engaging zone, in the most seamless and lean way.

Index

ABOUT THE AUTHOR

Shil Niyogi has helped many entrepreneurial firms streamline their existing operations to drive profitability. Currently, he is consulting on various product management assignments with entrepreneurial firms. His book *How Some Small Businesses Get their Ducks In A Row And Grow* was published by SAGE in 2011 and received excellent feedback from leading management leaders.

Shil went to the prestigious Delhi Technological University for his Civil Engineering undergrad, where he started the Creative Arts Society to cater to the innovators there. He started his career as a risk engineer. He studied the emerging insurance market there and its relevance to the Indian economy and wrote a series of articles for *The Economic Times*, a leading financial newspaper.

He received his MBA at UCLA Anderson School of Management, specializing in entrepreneurship and marketing. At Anderson, he revived the Operations Association, and also cofounded a student-run newsjournal on new management styles and innovations, for distribution to entrepreneurs. Currently, he continues to work with entrepreneurs and innovators to more effectively manage operations and service customers better, through enhanced intelligence gathering methods.